Ten Things I Learned from

BILL PORTER

Ten Things I Learned from

BILL PORTER

SHELLY BRADY

Foreword by William H. Macy

HODDER
MOBIUS

Hodder & Stoughton

First published by New World Library, USA, in 2002

First published in Great Britain in 2003 by Hodder and Stoughton
A division of Hodder Headline

1 3 5 7 9 10 8 6 4 2

ISBN 0 340 73443

A CIP catalogue record for this title is available
from the British Library

Printed and bound in Great Britain by
Clays Ltd, St Ives plc

Hodder and Stoughton
A division of Hodder Headline
338 Euston Road
London NW1 3BH

To

John,
Michelle, Katrina, Teressa,
Kevin, Erica, Emily,
Irene,
and Bill

CONTENTS

FOREWORD BY WILLIAM H. MACY

If memory serves, I was on the phone yelling at the concierge about his tardiness in delivering a fax to my room as I put the videotape that my agent had sent me into the machine. It was the *20/20* piece about Bill Porter. The tape was only about eight minutes long, but by the end, I stood in my hotel room with the remote still in my hand, and wept like a baby. I wept for his dignity. I wept for his stoicism. And mostly I wept for his indomitable optimism. Later that day I showed the piece to my wife, and we held each other and wept. I then sent the tape to my writing partner Steven Schachter. He wept. Steven and I decided we had to try to write a screenplay about Bill Porter.

In the process of researching Bill's life, we saw another tape of one of Bill's motivational speeches, which he delivered with the help of his assistant, Shelly Brady. As we watched Shelly, I said to Steven, "This story just gets better and better. She's a babe."

A month or so later, Steven and I flew to Portland to meet Shelly and Bill. Shelly picked us up at the airport, or more correctly, she swept us up at the airport. She had the same indomitable spirit and optimism as Bill. Thirty-six hours later, both Steven and I were smitten. She and Bill had that rare relationship: synchronicity of thought, ease of being, mutual respect, and joy in each other's company. I explored the possibility of being adopted by them.

I think I should let Shelly tell her story now. It's a great story. And, as everyone in Hollywood knows, a great story is always better if it has a babe in it.

October 2001
Los Angeles, California

Writers often speak of how their books wrote themselves, as if they were transcribing for a higher power. At times, while writing this book, I had a similar feeling. Each day before placing my fingers on the keyboard, I took a moment to ponder and pray, and then inspiration would come from above, leading me directly to Bill Porter himself. In spite of his cerebral palsy, he was able to overcome every obstacle he faced throughout his life and achieve all of his goals. Any momentary inability I had committing words to paper paled in comparison to the incredible challenges that Bill has met during his life.

Ideas about what should be in this book flowed from Bill; he was excited to participate and full of good stories. His answers to questions were succinct, yet rich in detail, as if he was in touch with that higher power that some writers allude to. Our chats struck just the right chords and triggered a flood of my own memories of our long friendship and, most importantly, of what I've learned from him.

Then again, much of the inspiration and driving force behind this book came from Bill Porter's fans. I've felt driven to introduce him to as many people as possible. I've seen and heard of many lives spiraling downward — physically, mentally, and spiritually — that suddenly improved when they read about Bill in the newspaper, saw him on a segment of ABC's *20/20,* or met him at one of our speaking engagements.

A common response to Bill's story is, "He made it through hardships I never dreamed of. What am I complaining about?" Admittedly, I had similar thoughts while juggling my role of mother to six children and writing this book, but visits with Bill always recharged me and kept me writing.

I met Bill when I was seventeen years old and still in high school. I walked into the school's administration office and my eyes were inexplicably attracted to a slip of paper tacked to the bulletin board. It read: *Delivery Person Wanted. Every other Saturday. Must supply own car. Please call Bill Porter at xxx-xxxx.* I thought I already had a great summer job lined up, but something inside me said I must have this one. It sounded like a dream come true for a teenager, and it was! I cruised around in the family car, listened to the radio, delivered products, and made money. I even liked Bill Porter; he was a nice, hard-working man who paid me much better than the minimum wage.

Curious customers would ask, "What's wrong with Bill? Does he have MS or muscular dystrophy or what?"

At the time, I didn't know and I didn't know how to ask him. Besides, it really didn't matter to me because our relationship was friendly and profitable. Why risk one of the best summers of my life asking a question that might offend him?

Years later, after college and the birth of my first child, Bill's delivery person gave notice and he inquired about my whereabouts. I was flattered that he remembered me and wanted me back, and the extra money certainly would come in handy. Sure enough, our lives became inexplicably intertwined, and for more than twenty years we've watched each other fall down and get back up many times, all the better for the experience. Every time our lives hit a rut, Bill was there for me and I was there for him.

Often, if Bill wasn't physically with me during times of trouble, he was there in my thoughts, and somehow just thinking of him renewed me. I'd remember all he'd been through and how he turned negative situations into positive ones. Simply thinking of Bill lifted me, refreshed me, and allowed me to believe that I, too, could achieve my goals. I've talked to many fans of Bill who describe a similar phenomenon when they reflect on who he is and all he's accomplished despite his challenges. In this book, I hope to share the lessons I've learned from Bill Porter, so you may know him, too.

Follow Your Passion

"**H**appy birthday to you! Happy birthday to you! Happy birthday, dear Bill! Happy birthday to you!"

I have never heard it sung so sincerely and by so many people. The entire audience at the John F. Kennedy Center in Washington, D.C. stood on their feet and applauded the sixty-sixth birthday of a most unsuspecting hero — Mr. Bill Porter, a door-to-door salesman for Watkins Products. Bill was all smiles as the clapping reverberated throughout the great hall. I, Shelly Brady, close friend and assistant to Bill, stood to his left; on his right stood another American hero, former astronaut and Senator John Glenn. The occasion was the presentation of an achievement award from the National Council on Communicative Disorders (and Bill's birthday, of course).

Bill won the award because he managed to succeed in business despite having cerebral palsy, a condition that greatly affects his speech and the muscles in his arms and legs. Listeners must pay close attention to Bill when he speaks because his vocal chords release words in a halting pattern. Resist the temptation to finish sentences for him, however, because if one is patient the words do come and are well worth waiting for, especially if Bill is knocking on your front door with attaché case in hand. Bill was chosen for the award because he embodies the dreams, the spirit, and the hope of individuals with communication disabilities or diseases.

Was that the greatest moment in Bill Porter's life?

The convention center in downtown San Francisco echoed with the cheers of seven thousand men and women from fifty-six countries. They shouted one word in unison — a name, understood in all of the fourteen languages spoken here: "Bill, Bill, Bill, Bill." The stage lights were bright and Bill couldn't see their faces or their tears of joy, but he felt the emotion and the love of the audience, all members of the Million-Dollar Roundtable. They represented the cream of the crop in the insurance and financial planning industries. When the cheers stopped, I spoke for about ten minutes on Bill's behalf because of his speech difficulties. The applause that followed lasted as long as the speech. Bill looked at me, as if asking for an idea as to when the standing ovation might end and what we should do in the meantime. I shrugged my shoulders and whispered, "Let's relish the moment."

Was that the greatest moment Bill Porter ever experienced?

The make-up girl applied powder to a shiny spot on the top of Bill's head. When ABC's *20/20* called about doing a segment on Bill, I nearly fell out of my chair. Here we were, a door-to-door salesman and his assistant, going about our rather mundane, day-to-day existence struggling to make ends meet, and all of a sudden ABC news correspondent Bob Brown is sitting across from us with the cameras rolling. Bill couldn't believe it when he found out that *20/20* had more than twenty million viewers. We were told the broadcast could change our lives. Companies would want him to share his story at their yearly conventions. I was wondering if there was a book or a movie in the future. Bill took it all in stride, only half-believing that the public exposure would help his sales; he knew that one-on-one sales work best. He was more interested in knowing, "Will I ever get to meet Barbara Walters?"

Was this the goal that Bill Porter had dreamed of?

The telephone rang. It was the personal assistant to the actor William H. Macy calling. Macy and writer-director Steven Schachter wanted to fly to Portland to meet in person with Bill Porter and myself. After three long years of hard work and a handful of rejections, TNT was ready to produce a movie based on the life of Bill Porter. Bill Macy, an Academy Award–nominated actor, co-wrote the script and planned to portray Bill in the docudrama. I picked up Mr. Macy and Mr. Schachter at the Portland Airport, and since I'm a big fan  of Macy's, I was trembling by the time they walked off the airplane. Soon, however, we were chatting like old friends. Then it was off to Bill Porter's house, where the two Bills met face to face. Macy extended his right hand to Bill, a gesture that was gladly accepted. To me, this handshake symbolized the great respect the two men held for each other. In an instant, I knew Macy was the right actor to portray Porter, and the sincere bonding between the two men brought tears to my eyes.

Was this the most exciting day in Bill Porter's life?

The palm trees swayed in the late afternoon breeze at the La Quinta Resort, a desert oasis outside Palm Springs, California. My pale skin was getting some color as we lounged by the pool, sipping virgin pina coladas.

"It doesn't get much better than this," Bill said to me as he adjusted his hat to keep the sun off his face.

We were unwinding after giving a motivational speech to a few hundred conventioneers. It went well, and I figured Bill was finally getting used to life on the road. No more wet dreary winters in Portland, Oregon, slip-sliding his way up steep driveways and staircases. *So this is what it's like to be rich and famous,* I was thinking; *I can handle this. I just need to figure the logistics of how I'm going to travel from resort to resort with six children and a husband in tow.* Bill brought me back

to reality when he asked, "How many messages do you think are on my answering machine? I mean, how many orders? Some of those people are going to buy their products at a warehouse store if I don't get back soon."

"I doubt it," I said. "Those customers are loyal to you."

"Exactly," Bill replied. "Loyal to *me,* not an answering machine."

Today, for medical reasons, Bill's travel is limited and La Quinta is only a fond memory, but he often speaks of that trip to Southern California. He says he can close his eyes and feel the warm sun on his skin and hear the wind rustling through the palm leaves.

Was this what he had looked forward to doing all of his life?

Bill spent years pounding the pavement, knocking on doors, ignoring rejection after rejection. No matter what response he received after knocking, no answers or negative replies, he moved

on, undaunted, for Bill had a mantra that calmed his nerves:
"The next house will say 'yes.' The next house will say 'yes.'"

Bill repeated this chant over and over as he trudged up
the hills of northwest Portland, approaching each house optimistically even if it was the same house that last month told
him, "How many times do I have to tell you? Never, ever
come back!" He'd go back again, month after month, with a
fresh and confident attitude. It was all a part of his strategy,
a strategy all good salespeople know about: wear them down
until they tire of saying "no." Eventually, they will buy.
Eventually, everyone buys.

Such positive thoughts constantly course through Bill's
mind and body. *Did they just say something about not coming
back? I must not have heard them correctly.*

After months and sometimes years of knocking on their
doors, Bill finally breaks them down. First, he hears a hint of
resignation in their voice. Next, they invite him in. Then,
they agree to look at his catalog. And finally, it's "I'll take one
of those." They may only order one bottle of vanilla this
time, but it's a sale, a sale from someone who once told him,
"No. Don't ever come back."

Was that the greatest moment? Yes, you bet it was.

When Bill is "cold calling" at a stranger's front door, he is in
his element. This is the moment he lives for: not knowing who
will answer, what their response will be, what mood they'll be
in. But most importantly, he wonders this: Will I make a sale?

Of his more than five hundred regular customers, Bill says that about thirty-five of them told him to never ever come back. They are among his best customers today.

Bill Porter has a passion for selling. His dream is to be number one. If there is one thing I have learned from him, it's that anyone can follow their passion and live their dream. Bill has proven to me that dreams have a way of coming true if we stay focused on the path, no matter what obstacles confront us.

Selling is Bill's life; he takes it with him wherever he goes. When companies first called wanting Bill to share his story with their employees, he had absolutely no interest. At first, I thought it was because he was embarrassed by his difficulty communicating. I later learned that he was uncomfortable not because of his speech impediment, but because speaking to a large audience wasn't his "style." He told me that he was a salesman from the old school, a one-on-one type of guy.

I, however, was very interested! Since I was a theater major in college, this was right up my alley.

"Wait a minute," I said. "Don't say no. We can do this speaking gig together."

Reluctantly, Bill agreed to give it a try for my sake. What disturbed Bill more than stage fright was that the speaking engagements would cut into his door-to-door sales. Our first speech was scheduled for a Saturday.

"No way," Bill said. "Saturday is callback day." That's the day he telephones customers that weren't home during the previous week. I suggested that he double up and do callbacks the next weekend. After all, he was his own boss.

"Absolutely not," he said. "Period."

I tried another angle that I thought might work with him.

"Bill," I said, "suppose you make more money on Saturday from the speaking fee than if you stayed home and did callbacks?" He still wasn't swayed. Then it dawned on me.

"Bill," I asked, "what if we handed out catalogs to all three hundred audience members and invited them to be your customers? You could potentially double your sales next month." Bingo! I could see Bill calculating the sales figures in his head. And as it turned out, dozens of audience members purchased items from Bill after our talk.

Everywhere we go, Bill makes new friends and customers (these two words are synonymous to Bill). The first time we traveled abroad we were scheduled to fly to Calgary to speak to Bill's own company, Watkins, Inc. The morning of our departure, a nagging thought kept crossing my mind. The night before, just before he dozed off, my husband asked, "Does Bill have picture ID?"

The question kept haunting me the next morning as I packed, said good-bye to the children, and caught a ride to the airport. Always prompt, Bill was waiting for me when I arrived. Together, we walked up to the ticket counter and presented our tickets. Then my nightmare came true. The agent asked, "May I see picture ID, please?"

"Here is my ID," I said. "However, my friend here has never driven a car. And, uh, well, therefore, he doesn't have picture ID."

Bill's fingers fumbled through his wallet searching for

anything with a picture on it. Credit cards, bus passes, and various receipts soon littered the ticket counter. Finally, he held up his library card with the innocence of a child.

The agent was briefly amused, but quickly regained his composure and asked, "Does Mr. Porter have a passport or a birth certificate?"

"Yeah, but not with him," I said. "Say, do you subscribe to the *Oregonian?* You do? Great! Then you must know who this man is. He's the Bill Porter in the 'Life of a Salesman' article, the man born with cerebral palsy. The man who was told by the State of Oregon that he was unemployable, and who went on to become the top salesman for Watkins Products. We have to get him to Canada to tell his story to conventioneers. Look at the picture of him on the cover of this magazine; underneath it says 'Bill Porter.' Doesn't that count as picture ID?"

The agent said he'd be right back; he had to speak to his supervisor. Bill and I stood nervously at the counter strumming our fingers and casting apologetic looks at the disgruntled travelers behind us.

Finally, the agent came back and said, "We can let you go to Canada, but you wouldn't be able to get back into the country without proof of citizenship." That could be a real problem for my husband and children, I thought. The ticket agent continued, "If you can secure proper documentation, we have a later flight."

We headed straight to a phone booth where I called the office of Vital Statistics in San Francisco, Bill's birthplace.

After waiting on hold for ten minutes, I finally got a voice. "Yes, we can locate William Douglas Porter's birth certificate, but it will take three weeks to process. No, it can't be faxed. No, there's nothing we can do to satisfy the agents at the airport. Sorry." Click.

I chanted another of Bill's mantras, "I have no obstacles," as we hailed a cab and headed to Bill's house. We tore through drawers and closets. Old family photos distracted us from our mission of finding picture ID for Bill. "Look how beautiful your mother looks in this photograph. She was so pretty," I sighed. Quit gabbing and keep looking, I reminded myself.

At last, underneath a pile of scrapbooks, we found a worn paper bag with the word *Statistics* written in red letters. I dumped the contents on the floor and we sorted through them: death certificate for Ernest Porter, marriage certificate for Bill's parents, life insurance policy, old electric bills. Finally, something appeared with the words *William Douglas Porter* on it...a baptismal certificate. Maybe, just maybe, this would work.

I shoved everything into the bag and called a cab that took us to the Department of Motor Vehicles. After a twenty-minute wait in line, we stepped up to the counter. I placed the *Statistics* bag on the counter next to the magazine with Bill's picture on the cover. I pleaded our case.

"We missed our plane and we have to go to Canada. This is the famous Bill Porter and he needs picture ID."

I was just warming up when the DMV lady interrupted me.

"Oh, you're the man featured in the *Oregonian* article. I read that story and I couldn't stop crying." She paused a moment and looked at the documents on the counter in front of her. "What's this? You have only one piece of identification, your baptismal certificate. Hmm, you're really supposed to have two pieces of identification. If you promise not to tell a soul, I don't think there is any question who you are. Honey, you just come on back here and I'll take your picture. I'll have you on that plane in no time." Somehow, while I organized all the paperwork, Bill managed to sell his new friend/customer a can of Watkins cinnamon.

If Bill told you his version of this story, it would go something like this: *Once we missed a plane because I didn't have ID. Missing the plane didn't bother me at all; missing a day of selling is what annoyed me. Fortunately, all was not lost. The nice lady at the DMV bought a can of cinnamon and took a catalog to share with her family and friends. Boy, am I glad I didn't have picture ID; just think of all the new business I got. I wish Shelly would have calmed down; she looked like she was ready to pass out.*

Bill Porter is a perfect example of an individual succeeding because he stayed focused on something he felt passionate about. Like his father, Bill's passion was for selling, to be the best salesman he could be without compromising his values. Bill once received a ten-minute standing ovation at the end of one of our speeches when he passionately urged audience members to simply "go out there and make it happen." Following my passion was one of the first things I learned from Bill.

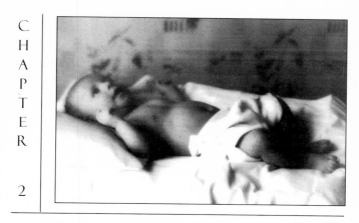

It Doesn't Matter How You Got Here, Only Where You're Going

September 9, 1932, was the happiest day in the lives of Ernest and Irene Porter. The time was 2:20 A.M. and they were the proud parents of a baby boy, William Douglas Porter. In spite of the difficult labor (the doctor had to use forceps to extract baby Bill), Irene would have gladly repeated the experience for what they received that morning: a precious and healthy little boy. The birth certificate on the table was proof of that; on line 29, under the heading "Congenital Crippling Deformities," was typed the word "None."

I picture Irene with baby Bill in her arms during the first few months of his life, when no signs of cerebral palsy were evident. I see her counting ten fingers and ten toes, caressing his soft skin, and gently running her fingers over the handsome features of his face. He seemed perfect in every way.

It didn't take long, though, before she knew something

was wrong. She knew it before anyone else. Bill's perfectly shaped left hand was always clenched ever so tightly. Irene also noticed that her infant son's back was arched and stiff. She spent hours massaging his shoulders and back. She gently pried his fingers open, only to see them revert back into a tight little fist.

On her own, Irene researched the stages of child development and discovered that Bill's growth was not proceeding normally. He wasn't strong enough to roll over, sit up, or crawl. He wasn't strong enough to hold the bottle on his own. Irene read every book she could find on child development, which, at the time, were few and far between. One book recommended what's called the "parachute test," whereby a baby is held level and face down, two feet over the bed, and dropped. By six months of age the baby should instinctively protect itself by spreading its arms and legs to ease the fall. Bill just plopped down on the bed without the slightest sign of self-protection.

Irene carefully watched the progress of infants of friends and relatives; she tried to objectively compare them to Bill's development. Shortly before Bill's first birthday, she couldn't deceive herself anymore; Bill was not performing as he should. She couldn't ignore the fact that Bill still clenched his left hand no matter how many times she tried to uncurl it. The hour-long massages weren't working the magic she hoped on Bill's poor posture. There was no denying that Irene and Ernest must seek a professional opinion.

Irene pointed out Bill's physical problems to the family

doctor. The doctor immediately recognized the symptoms and diagnosed cerebral palsy. Suddenly, life was a whirlwind of doctors, therapists, and experts. Little was known about cerebral palsy in the 1930s, but most of the specialists suggested that Bill had no hope for a normal life. They predicted he would be mentally retarded and suggested he be placed in an institution. The Porters were appalled at the idea of their precious baby being torn from their lives. Irene knew in her heart that Bill was bright and intelligent. She vowed to do everything in her power to understand and conquer the illness that crippled her son.

Helping her son grow up to become the very best he could became her sole mission in life, *her passion.* No other children would be born in the Porter household; Ernest and

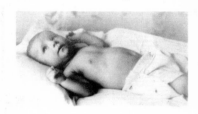

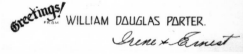
Greetings! FROM WILLIAM DOUGLAS PORTER.
Irene & Ernest

Irene needed every bit of time and energy they could muster to ensure that Bill was well taken care of. They devoted their lives to Bill and never looked back.

Over the years, Bill asked his mother many times to repeat the story of his birth. She said, "It was a difficult labor that lasted far too long and everyone was afraid neither you nor I would make it. The doctor needed to use forceps because you were stuck in the birth canal. The very forceps that saved your life also damaged a section of your brain. That's why you have a difficult time using your muscles.

None of that matters now; what matters is where you're going, not how you got here."

Bill had no idea of the pain Ernest and Irene felt upon the revelation that their son had cerebral palsy. Family members tell of the sadness they felt. Many tears were shed, and sometimes the questions "Why Bill?" and "Why us?" were asked. There never was a clear answer; they accepted it as part of God's plan. A close friend of the family recalls "The Porters were initially devastated when they learned that Bill had cerebral palsy, but it was only for a brief spell. Bill was their treasure, their gift from God."

Ernest quit his steady job as a salesman, a frightening prospect for anyone during the Great Depression, let alone someone with a child with a disability. He searched for work that would help him better understand and treat his son's disability. He found work with the Berry School in San Francisco, an educational institution for handicapped children. He worked in the physical therapy department and young Bill would often accompany his father to work. Bill fondly remembers trying on the "duck shoes," long boards roped to the feet of children who needed assistance in straightening their walk. Throughout the next decade, Ernest and Irene Porter worked at various locations of the Berry School — San Francisco, Los Angeles, Phoenix, and Chicago — wherever their services were needed.

Irene worked as a cook for the school. Her salary made up for the pay cut Ernest took when he left sales work. Ernest and Irene assisted Bill with exercises that greatly improved his muscle coordination. They also assisted Bill every evening with speech therapy. Bill learned quickly; his ability and will to communicate increased in leaps and bounds. Bill quickly proved naysayers wrong; his mental capabilities were normal. They were all on a long arduous journey, one that would determine whether Bill would stay with them or enter an institution.

No one except Bill really knew how he felt about his disability, if he felt inferior because he was different from the other children. Bill says he doesn't remember thinking negatively about his condition. He is blessed with inheriting a philosophy from his parents that believes in focusing on the future, not dwelling on the past. The past is something the Porter family learned from, not doted over. To Bill, his cerebral  palsy is yesterday's news, something that isn't worth rehashing, and he doesn't want anyone else focusing on it either.

Several years after Bill and I first met, I finally got the courage to ask him about his condition. Although he set me straight about his cerebral palsy, his comments were short and to the point and the subject was not brought up again for another decade.

"I was just wondering," I asked awkwardly, "I mean, some of your customers, well, I wondered what you have. I mean is it MS or cerebral palsy or what?"

Bill matter-of-factly answered, "I have cerebral palsy."

I am rarely at a loss for words, but I continued to stumble forward. "What does that mean? How did you get it? Will it get worse?"

Bill replied, "I was born with cerebral palsy. My mother told me a doctor's instrument — forceps — damaged a section of my brain at birth. My condition will never get any worse, nor will it get any better. What you see is what you get. It's not a big deal. It's part of my past and it doesn't bother me. It doesn't stop me from accomplishing whatever I set my mind to . . . which happens, at this moment, to be doing well with the Watkins collection and doing even better in two weeks."

After doing some research on my own, I learned that cerebral palsy is frequently caused by a lack of oxygen to the brain, most often occurring during childbirth. Fortunately, accidents like the one that happened to Bill during childbirth are becoming rarer because of modern medical technology. Organizations such as United Cerebral Palsy have funded research into its causes and prevention. Pre- and post-natal care have greatly lowered the incidence of CP. I have often wondered if the forceps didn't damage his brain but instead saved his life since Bill might have been stuck in the birth canal, unable to breathe. Then I remember that it's senseless to ponder about Bill's CP; I must put it in the past, as Bill has.

As hard as I try, I just can't put myself in Bill's shoes. I can't comprehend how he maintains his optimism, how he enthusiastically gets out of bed on the coldest, dreariest mornings imaginable and prepares to hit the pavement. He has done this daily with vigor for more than thirty years. Every morning Bill's alarm rings at 4:45 A.M. so he has time to get ready to catch the 7:20 A.M. bus to downtown Portland. Bill needs this much time to look his best; he doesn't like to dress in a rush. He believes that appearance is essential in sales, especially in door-to-door sales where customers invite you into their homes.

And so the wee hours of Bill's mornings are filled with the painstaking process of dressing. His left hand doesn't help much with the putting on of socks, trousers, white shirt, blazer, and, finally, wing tip shoes. He always leaves the cuffs unbuttoned and his shoelaces loose. Occasionally, he has managed to accomplish these tasks alone, but usually they take too much time. Better, he has decided, to acknowledged his needs and ask friends at a downtown hotel for a little help.

In the past after Bill's best efforts, Irene would tighten his shoelaces, button his cuffs and collar, and clip his tie on. She would cook him a warm breakfast and pack him a lunch. That allowed more time for Bill to organize his paperwork and read the newspaper. For decades, Bill and Irene followed the same routine until she became ill with Alzheimer's. With much trepidation, Bill followed the doctor's advice and placed her in adult foster care and eventually in a nursing home. That's when Bill had to start relying on others to help him. Not being the most adept cook in the world, he learned to enjoy a breakfast of cold cereal and toast. He paid a neighbor to pack him a lunch.

Irene was a perfectionist when it came to housekeeping. When she was gone, Bill maintained her high standards: the bath towels were neatly folded and hung on the towel bar just so, the shrubbery was trimmed regularly, and the lawn edged, not just mowed.

After getting help with his buttons, laces, and tie from the hotel bellhops, he was ready to catch the 8:30 bus to the West Hills, one of the better neighborhoods of Portland. Bill earned this prime territory by outselling other representatives of Watkins products.

It is now 9:00 A.M., more than four hours since Bill arose, and

he finally steps off the bus to begin his workday. Door after door he approaches, knocks or rings, and waits for an answer. He doesn't skip any houses on the presumption that no car in the driveway means nobody is home. Who knows? The car might be in the shop. Undaunted by no answer at most of the doors, Bill continues on, body slightly bent forward, left hand clutching a briefcase, right hand clenched in a fist behind him. His hat is squarely on his head, rain or shine. Often he wears a trench coat with a removable liner that is taken out in the spring and summer.

An eye checks out Bill through a peephole. He knows they are home, but they still don't answer. Other times, without even opening the door, he hears "No thank you." "I'm not inter-ested." "I gave to charity last month." "We don't want any." "Go away." No after no after no, Bill treks on until at last some-one is cordial and invites him in. Amazingly, the rejections don't bother him. They are all erased by a single order. Like a mantra, Bill repeats over and over to himself, "The next cus-tomer will say yes, the next customer will say yes." Eventually, Bill believes, they all will say "yes." He just has to be patient.

There have been a few very low points in Bill's life. A number of years ago, he was having a tough time making financial ends meet and became easy prey for a mortgage company soliciting his business over the phone. He signed up for an extremely expensive interest refinance package that nearly cost him his house. Because of the huge monthly pay-ments, he had to cancel his medical insurance. Shortly there-after, he had to have major back surgery. Between the medical bills and high house payments, Bill was almost forced into bankruptcy. It is only very recently, with the increased sales that occurred after the *20/20* show aired, that Bill has been able to pay off some of the loans and keep abreast of his medical expenses.

Bill made another financial blunder when he accepted an inflated estimate for work on his house. The company installed two basement windows and charged him $2,000. Fortunately, I happened to see the invoice on his table and questioned Bill about it.

"Did you get two or three estimates?" I asked.

"No, they seemed honest," was the reply.

I have come to believe an old saying: Sales people are the easiest people to sell to. I called the construction company and spoke to the owner, who acknowledged a billing error. He lowered the cost to a more reasonable $800. Now I try to scrutinize the bills on Bill's table before he pays them since he is incapable of adopting a suspicious attitude toward others. He always tells the truth to his clients: when they can expect delivery, what the total cost will be, and how the "satisfaction guaranteed" policy works. Since Bill never tells a lie, he assumes that others have the same regard for honesty that he does. When Bill and I were first trying to establish ourselves as inspirational speakers we were very naive. Early on we got an inquiry from a company on the East Coast. They didn't want us to go to the trouble of traveling — or so they said — and would gladly send a crackerjack team of journalists out to interview us in Portland. More than likely, they didn't want to go to the expense of flying us to their convention and putting us up in a hotel. I also knew the videotape wouldn't be as powerful as a live on-stage performance, but I didn't know how to convince them of the fact.

Well, before I knew it, the whole crew was at Bill's house. They interviewed and videotaped him without any monetary compensation. The video was then shown at their yearly convention to entertain and inspire the employees. I kept checking the mailbox, expecting some sort of compensation or at least a thank you note, but nothing arrived. To make matters worse, I misplaced the name of the company and wasn't able to let them know how I felt about what they had done.

For months, I was burned up that a company would take advantage of our innocence. They knew speakers at business conventions are to be compensated, whether it is a live presentation or a videotaped one. I wasted a lot of time and energy fuming over this obvious wrongdoing. In fact, my anger and distrust were hampering the promotion of Bill and my new enterprise.

Bill took it all in stride; he was more interested in his next sale of Watkins Products. Finally, I followed his example and started believing that most companies are reputable and will pay fairly for our time and efforts. Eventually, we placed our trust in an agency that represents speakers. Now, little details such as getting paid for a speech are handled professionally. Who says Shelly can't learn a new attitude, can't learn from the past and yet leave it behind and live for the present and the future?

You see, I'm trying to apply Bill's way of living to my personal life. For a long time, I've carried a few bitter memories from my childhood. Raised by my mother and a physically abusive stepfather, I have sometimes bemoaned my less than ideal childhood. To this day, many of my brothers and sisters struggle with the effects of growing up in a dysfunctional family. With Bill as a role model, I am trying to accept the past and go forward. Occasionally, I lose my temper and can trace it directly back to painful experiences I had as a child, when my stepfather would burst into a fit of rage for no reason. Heaven forbid that I should subject my husband or children to ranting of that sort.

A lot of good things happened in my life, too. Eventually,

my "wicked" stepfather changed: my family moved to Hawaii (that was rough!), joined a church, and adopted three children. Eventually, we moved back to Oregon where I met Bill Porter, then I met my husband and we created six amazing children. Life is beautiful.

If I could go back and change anything about my life, I wouldn't. I have come to realize that everything that's ever happened to me, both good and bad, has shaped me into who I am today.

Sometimes, I have days that are hard. I find myself reverting to past behavior patterns. I raise my voice impatiently or avoid helping someone. I make excuses to myself for my inappropriate actions: "I'm tired." "I had a rough day." "The house is a mess." Lately, I've been able to stop, turn myself around, and say, "It doesn't matter how I got to this point or where I am at this moment, only where I'm headed." I am learning to lower my voice and help children and friends in need.

Someone once said that it's better to be four feet from the mouth of hell headed toward heaven than to be four miles away from heaven headed toward hell. There are no fence sitters. You are either moving forward or backward. I think of my friend Bill, who in the past six decades has had his share of hard days. He knows his back will feel better, his migraine will go away, and he'll be able to catch his breath. It always happens. It always will.

CHAPTER 3

Mother Knows Best

I shudder at the thought of how easily Bill's life could have turned out very differently, and how close we all came to not having the pleasure of knowing Bill Porter. The reason we know him boils down to one moment in time, more than half a century ago, a moment when a simple "yes" or "no" determined his fate. Instead of following the adamant advice of doctors, friends, and family and entering little Bill into an institution, his mother Irene made the decision to raise her son at home. She said, "Bill is my baby, my child. I will raise him," and stuck by her vow, for better or worse, in sickness and in health, for richer or poorer, rather than subject him to a life of lonely misery in a place where people don't get better.

Without taking anything away from Bill, the character traits that we most admire in him can be directly linked to his mother. It's difficult to imagine raising a child with cerebral palsy in the 1930s. Today there are high-tech wheelchairs, advanced prosthetic devices, and miracle drugs. Associations devoted to integrating the handicapped into mainstream society have helped make it illegal to discriminate against or inhibit physical access to individuals with disabilities. We are now more accustomed to seeing and interacting with mentally and physically challenged individuals than ever before.

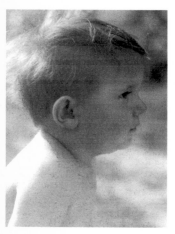

Back when Bill was a child, no such technological or sociological advancements were in place. It was extremely difficult for handicapped individuals to maneuver in stores and places of employment, let alone apartments and schools. At the same time, the social stigma attached to being handicapped could be devastating to an individual and their family. If a family decided to raise their "different" child at home, he or she was often hidden away from public view; poor education and rehabilitation often followed.

Irene Porter didn't buy into society's treatment of the handicapped; she rebelled against the prevailing attitude toward the disabled. She was a formidable foe to anyone who dared treat Bill as a lesser person because he had cerebral palsy. Her persistence and stubbornness is legendary among friends, family, and school administrators.

Bill, like other similarly challenged children, wasn't allowed in a public school until he graduated from an institution for the handicapped. Irene vociferously opposed this discriminatory rule; she saw absolutely no reason why Bill couldn't attend. Unfortunately, the school district won the battle, and Bill was forced to graduate from the Grout School for Handicapped Children before he could attend Lincoln High School in Portland, where Irene promptly enrolled him when he reached the age of sixteen. Although Bill got a good education at Grout School, Irene felt it was important for him to receive a diploma from a public school if he was to get a decent job. Her determination and stubbornness paid off four years later when Bill graduated in a cap and gown at his high school graduation ceremony. He was a model student

Lincoln High School

Portland, Oregon

This certifies that

WILLIAM DOUGLAS PORTER

has completed the Required Course of Study as prescribed by the Board of Directors.

Given by School District Number One, Multnomah County, Oregon, on the 11th day of June, in the year of our Lord nineteen hundred and fifty-four.

A. Eugene Allen
Chairman of the Board of Directors

J.W. Edwards
Superintendent of Schools

Glen F. Wiest
Principal

who paved the way for other handicapped students to enter public schools.

Irene knew that anything was possible if one is patient and persistent. She actually wrote the word "persistence" on slips of paper and secretly hid them in Bill's pockets or lunch bag for him to find later. Bill recalls a time in high school when he was trying his best to get an interview with the high school coach after the football team won a championship game in overtime. Bill kept getting nudged aside by celebratory players and supporters. He was ready to give up and write the story without the one-on-one interview. On his reporter's notebook he noticed the words "Persistence pays off." Bill laughed aloud as he told me this story. Irene was up to her old tricks, but it kept Bill pressing on, which eventu-

ally got him a great interview with the coach that was featured in the next issue of the school paper.

Another character trait that Bill learned from his mother was neatness. Bill's customers are often surprised by how sharp he looks when making his route. Even though many of them are his friends now, Bill still dresses formally because he

feels if he dressed more casually his sales might go down. I know where he got this passion for good grooming — Irene. Even on a tight budget she was a fastidious dresser; her blouses and skirts were always cleaned, pressed, and fashionable. Irene demanded the same of her son no matter how long it took him to dress. For years, Bill's fingers would trip over themselves as he practiced tying his shoelaces over and over again. His best efforts only got them tight enough to last a few minutes. Nevertheless, you can bet that before he approached his mother for help, he had done his best. Only then would she kneel down and tie them tighter. In fact, Irene was always willing to make the final buttoning of collars and cuffs, but otherwise her son was required to completely dress himself. Bill remembers the routine well:

"I had to wake up very early as a little boy, before my

dad, even before the sun would rise. It took that much longer for me to get dressed. In the quiet stillness of the morning, I would struggle. My mom would busy herself with packing lunches and cooking breakfast. I learned to make my bed, pick up after myself, and get dressed just like every other child in the neighborhood."

Irene managed to keep herself and her family well dressed because she was an excellent shopper. Once when I opened the clothes dryer at Bill's house, out tumbled six shirts with identical pinstripes. I asked him "Why don't you mix up your wardrobe a little and buy slightly different colored shirts? Maybe a beige one or a yellow one?"

"I didn't buy those, mom did," he answered. "They were on sale at the department store. Nice shirts, aren't they? Look, the buttons never fall off and the stitches hold together."

I didn't pursue the conversation further, except to agree they were of good quality. By using coupons and following sales, Irene managed to keep Bill and her family appearing to live well beyond their means. She was also an attractive woman, and when she dressed up she could turn quite a few heads.

Irene's attention to detail also was evident in the appearance of her home. Bill was assigned the task of keeping the yard neat, which was overwhelming at times for a child with physical limitations. I once asked Bill if he could ever remember his mom getting upset with him.

"Sure," he said, "she got upset a fair amount, like any mother does, right?"

Because I become cranky occasionally myself, I was glad to hear Bill's mom wasn't perfect. I can only hope when my children are grown, time will soften their memories and they'll be hard pressed to remember mom's occasional loss of patience. I won't hold my breath.

I prodded him further, "Do you remember any specific time?" One time in particular stood out in his mind.

"It was a warm summer day," he recalled. "My chore was to mow the lawn, weed the flowerbeds, edge the yard, and

trim a few bushes. I started in the cool of the morning. After a lunch break, my mom inspected my progress and wasn't pleased. She thought I should have been nearly done, if not completely done before lunch. Instead, I'd hardly made a dent. This infuriated her so much she told me she was going to go take a nap, and that I'd better be done by the time she got up. Well, I wasn't done, and boy did she let me have it. She hollered and threw a real fit; she was so upset. She told me I was slow, too much of a perfectionist, and I'd have to stay right there in the yard and finish it even if it took all summer."

Bill insists to this day that he was working as fast as he could, but his mother hit the nail on the head when she accused him of being a perfectionist. Like mother, like son, you might say.

Bill always names his mother as his greatest inspiration. (His father played a much smaller role in Bill's life because he was gone much of the time, working as a salesman.) He thinks about his mother every day. On the days that are filled with pain or rejection, he keeps going, knowing she would be proud, knowing she loved him unconditionally. One of Irene's biggest worries was what would happen to Bill after she and Ernest were gone. She thus insisted that Bill learn to support himself and not depend on others. She wanted so much for him to be independent even though at times it contradicted her protective, motherly instincts. The Porters, like many families of that era, believed that hard work and determination could take you far. It was a lesson they passed on to Bill, and in his case it really paid off.

I can only imagine how Irene handled motherhood. When I became a mother, I was amazed by the little miracle in my arms, and at the same time overwhelmed. Nothing I learned in college prepared me for the awesome responsibility of parenthood. All I knew at that moment was I wanted to raise my children right and love them unconditionally, knowing someday I would have to let them go.

Six children later, I am still learning and discovering the ups and downs, the disappointments, and, most of all, the joys of motherhood. My dream is to see my children mature, find their own paths, and become productive members of society. Some days, especially when they are squabbling and carrying on, I want this to happen sooner rather than later. Other days, I wonder where the time has gone. Who is this child, only moments before cradled in my arms, now fifteen years old with a driver's permit, backing out of the garage and forgetting to open the garage door? Most days, I try to enjoy the journey. Heck, it seems like yesterday when it was *my* mom who was tolerant when I backed the family car into a fence.

The greatest lesson I learned from Irene, which I think about daily, is the knowledge that unconditional love does exist. I learned how much power it has over both oneself and others. This purest form of love transcends nationalities, religions, and physical appearances. It isn't dependent on performance, grades, or physical prowess. I believe that Irene continuously enveloped Bill in tremendous doses of this kind of love, and it was this gigantic, all-knowing energy that enabled him to make it through the rough spots in his life. Bill carries this love around with him all the time. It has helped him to dismiss the prejudices and obstacles that would knock even the best of us down.

Recently, I experienced this type of love when I dropped my daughter off at high school. My older children are going through the stage when it's embarrassing to be seen with their mother. Half the kids drive themselves to school and anything less isn't considered cool. She begs me to drop her off two blocks away on a side street. On one morning, I rebelled. As she was getting ready to exit my car, I said, "Wait a minute. This is ridiculous. What are we hiding from?"

She replied with a long, drawn out, "Mom, you just don't get it."

I countered, "I do get it. I love you and there is nothing wrong with that."

She stopped for a moment, rolled her eyes, and sighed. "I love you too, Mom. Next time, you can drop me right in front."

With that, she hopped out of the car and walked toward the school. My heart swelled and tears came to my eyes as I remembered the feelings of love I experienced when she was first laid in my arms. It's important to me that my children know I will always be there for them and will always love them unconditionally. Thank you, Irene, for your beautiful example.

Persistence Pays Off

Within days of Bill's extraordinary graduation from Lincoln High School in Portland, his father, Ernest, uttered three words that rang in Bill's head: "Get a job!" His father wasn't about to let Bill rest on his laurels. According to Ernest, the cap-and-gown affair was a significant achievement, but there was a real world out there, and he fully expected Bill to take an active and profitable role in it. To this day, when Bill repeats his father's strong words "Get a job," I sense the profound effect they had on his entire life. A little part of my motherly instinct disapproves of Bill's father acting so sternly and seemingly uncaring toward his disabled child, but another wiser part of me knows that Bill's father acted in the best possible way a parent can. I hope that I am as brave and unselfish when the time comes to set my children free to find their own paths.

Bill took his father's ultimatum to heart. However, his cerebral palsy shortened the list of employment possibilities. Gardening for neighbors seemed a logical choice; it didn't require the use of a car, and he always appreciated well-manicured yards. So Bill started knocking on doors and within one month he had a few yards under his care. He watered, mowed, and weeded, earning approximately four dollars a week, which seemed like a fair amount of money to Bill at the time.

Ernest thought yard work was below Bill, though, and rightfully so. Watering yards wasn't a real job, not for Bill; it wasn't fulfilling or challenging enough. Anybody could mow lawns. He agreed with his father. Besides, Bill wanted more human contact, not to mention higher wages. The fact was, he wasn't built for mowing, raking, and sweeping. Every work day ended in physical pain. His muscles contracted and his back stooped lower. He knew there had to be a better job out there, something that better satisfied his father and himself. Four dollars a week was fine if one lived at home for the rest of his life, but Bill had to consider that someday he would have to pay his own way and possibly care for his aging parents.

Bill's mother suggested that he consider being a salesman for United Cerebral Palsy. Irene had volunteered countless hours for the nonprofit organization throughout her lifetime. She hoped that one day a cure would be found. At the time, UCP was involved in a fundraising drive in which people with cerebral palsy sold various household items and earned a small commission. Irene knew the fundraiser worked and that it would be a great opportunity for Bill.

Bill jumped at the idea and soon was trekking throughout his neighborhood, knocking on doors, even approaching people on the streets and in parks. Customers must have liked Bill's enthusiasm for his products (and his life) because the nickels and dimes kept coming. He continued to water yards but avoided mowing them because he wanted to save his legs and back for sales work. After a few months, he was a top salesman for the local UCP affiliate. Finally, he felt like a contributing member of society. His father must have thought so, too, because he no longer told Bill to "Get a job."

After two profitable years of selling for UCP, Bill began to see a downturn in the market for his products; it was evident that customers could only use so many of the limited items he sold. In fact, Bill's best customers finally told him that they couldn't use even one more basket or potholder. Bill needed a product that was consumed or used up so he could get long-term repeat sales. He also realized that the hardest part of selling was developing a clientele who trusted and liked you.

"What a waste," he thought, "to develop all those good relationships with customers and not be able to sell them something they need on a regular basis."

Bill knew in his heart that he was a natural-born salesman; he simply needed the right product. Once again he brainstormed, searching for the perfect product to sell. As Bill explained to me, "The answer came to me as I noticed a mail order gift catalog my mother had been browsing through one day. Right in front of me was a booklet filled with products for sale. I flipped through the pages. There must have been at least a hundred different gifts. I wondered how I could sell these same items and make a profit. Then it hit me. It was so simple. I would cut out the pictures from the catalog, paste them on to construction paper, and then type in my own prices — higher, of course."

He didn't notice the hours and days slipping by as he cut, pasted, and typed each gift item, carefully creating a unique catalog for his sales venture. He wanted to make sure that if verbal communication broke down between himself and his clients due to his speech impediment, the illustrated catalog would do the explaining for him. Bill planned to visit his basket customers, his yard clients, and every home within a five-mile radius. He was hyped up to sell, sell, and sell again.

The venture paid off and Bill made more money than he ever had before. The fifties were a rosy decade for the Porter family. Ernest earned a comfortable living selling custom signs for the Ramsey Neon Sign Company. Bill had launched his own career as a salesman. Irene kept busy with household chores, the church, and volunteering for United Cerebral Palsy.

The sixties, however, were not so kind to the Porters. Ernest learned from his doctor that he had high cholesterol and should watch his diet. These early warnings from the doctor made Bill even more aware of his future responsibility as the main breadwinner in the family. The financial burden of caring for his father and mother began to weigh heavily upon his shoulders. He felt compelled to look for another job, possibly with a big name company, one that had health benefits and more opportunity for advancement.

Ernest never appeared sick and never missed a day of work, but Irene worried and fussed over him. He ignored the doctor's advice and continued to eat poorly. Bill knew it was only a matter of time before his family would have to make do on his meager income alone. But his gross pay of sixty-five dollars a month simply wouldn't keep food on the table. In the few free hours that Bill could spare each day, he searched for new and better employment. Thus began his daily trips to the Oregon State Department of Employment.

Every morning before his eight hours of selling would start, Bill took the bus downtown to meet with employment counselors. Day after day, week after week, month after month, he would walk the same blocks to stand in line behind dozens of other unemployed workers. Bill lists that experience as one of the most degrading and humiliating of his life.

Initially, the employment officers made a sincere effort to assist Bill. His attitude was excellent and his appearance was very presentable. When the position of stock clerk at a major pharmacy came up, they referred Bill. However, the cerebral palsy made his hands twitch in a most uncooperative way; he kept knocking the bottles and jars off the crowded shelves. Depressing as it was to be let go before his first day was out, Bill returned to the unemployment office the very next morning with his head held high and his shoes shined bright.

A few days later Bill's persistence paid off; another job offer appeared that seemed to be a perfect match. Goodwill Industries needed a cashier at one of their retail stores in downtown Portland. Bill was good with numbers and extremely honest. Unfortunately, his fingers wouldn't extend fully or respond accurately and he kept hitting the wrong keys. The manager of the store quickly lost patience with Bill's corrected register receipts, and he let Bill go three short days later.

Next, Bill was hired to work the docks at the Salvation Army, but it was soon obvious to everyone that Bill wasn't physically able to load the trucks. The well-meaning agents at the employment office finally realized that Bill couldn't be expected to perform well at jobs that required manual labor.

They told Bill they had found the right match and sent him to answer phones at the Veterans Rehabilitation Center. Bill couldn't figure out why anyone would hire him to do phone work considering his difficulties communicating, but he was willing to try anything they recommended. After all, they were the experts. After numerous complaints about Bill's slurred speech, he was let go from this job as well. With four job reports rubber-stamped with "Unemployable" in Bill Porter's file — the pharmacy, Goodwill Industries, Salvation Army, and the Veterans Rehabilitation Center — things were not looking up for Bill Porter's employability. His handicap was too limiting.

The agents at the state employment office were cordial to Bill, but daily they came back with the same depressing news: "Sorry Bill, nothing today." Bill persevered day after day, week after week, and month after month. There simply was no work in which Bill's handicap wouldn't impair his performance. Finally, after five grueling months, an agent politely told him that he didn't need to come back. The state deemed him unemployable; they recommended he stay home and collect disability. The agent went on to tell Bill, "You have too much motivation for your own good." To say the least, Bill Porter did not take this as a compliment. He took it as a direct challenge to his self-worth, a personal challenge, as did his parents. He vowed to prove them wrong.

Bill stopped going to the employment office and decided to be his own employment counselor. That meant screening the Help Wanted ads of the Portland *Oregonian* on a daily basis. Everyday he would call a half dozen job possibilities. But most of the people he spoke to wouldn't let him complete the phone interview, let alone come in for a personal interview. Sometimes the company representative would harshly state that they weren't hiring as soon as they heard his speech impediment. He would often hear the abrupt click of a phone being hung up on him, but the dial tone only prompted Bill to call another ad.

Undaunted, Bill pressed on, ignoring any jobs that required manual labor. And then, like father, like son, he decided to focus on sales jobs. He knew he could sell; the experience with UCP had taught him that. One of the first companies he contacted was the Fuller Brush Company. He was amazed and his spirits soared when the local distributor said he would stop by for a personal interview. Bill relates the story this way:

"The Fuller Brush man came into my living room and before we even had a chance to talk much, he said the job wasn't for me. He had a black case with him — the product

bag — but told me I wouldn't be able to carry it. He didn't even ask me to try. He just took one look at me and assumed I couldn't do it. I knew he didn't want me. He wouldn't even give me a chance."

Bill and I have repeated this story at speaking engagements across the country. I always look at him when we're done — he gets a twinkle in his eye whenever he hears the story — and ask, "Have you ever noticed the Fuller Brush Company hasn't invited us to speak?" He quickly answers with a big grin and giggles. Bill's giggles are so sincere and so contagious that soon the entire auditorium is filled with laughter.

However, if a Fuller Brush representative, or a representative from any of the other companies that turned down Bill's services, is reading this, please don't be concerned. We realize that these incidents were a long time ago and that employment practices have changed considerably since Bill was turned away. We now know that most of those companies that rejected Bill wish he were on their team. And yes, we would welcome an invitation to share Bill's story with any and all of them, the Fuller Brush Company included!

So Bill ignored the rejections and called the next ad for a sales position — Watkins, Incorporated. They, too, agreed to interview Bill in person. This time Bill wasn't about to take "no" for an answer. He met the Watkins director's reluctance to hire him head on.

"I know I can do this job," he told him. "I've been successfully selling for the past ten years. It's in my blood. My father is a successful salesman. It almost doesn't matter what product I sell, customers enjoy buying from me."

Once again Bill waited for the rejection. It was only a matter of how it would come. Would it be the familiar "Don't call us, we'll call you" or "The position has already been filled"? The manager took his time. Finally, with great hesitation, he offered Bill the job, on a trial basis only. So what if it was the worst territory in Portland. It was a real job! It was a lot better than disability payments, and it was certainly better than mowing lawns.

Within a week of the job interview Bill had equipped himself with a briefcase filled with colorful catalogs and optimistically hit the streets of his new territory. His elation quickly turned to dismay, however, as he walked from house to house. The neighborhood was worse than he had imagined: caved-in porches, missing steps, handrails hanging by a nail. Most of the houses desperately needed paint and the yards were unkempt and overgrown. No wonder the manager gave him a crack! Since the job paid commissions only, the company had nothing to lose. Bill doubted if anyone had *ever* made a sale in this neighborhood. It was a wonder the United States Postal Service even delivered mail here. Forget that he wasn't going to make a dime; he might get hurt falling through a porch! Stubbornly unwilling to survive on disability payments, he climbed step after rickety porch step.

Rejection after rejection only made Bill more determined to prove he was employable, that he was a salesman. He would make his parents proud. Watkins wouldn't regret hiring Bill Porter. Still, he couldn't believe there were so many excuses for not buying a good product from a good salesman. "We're moving." "We don't have any money." "No soliciting." To Bill, every "no" simply meant that the first "yes" couldn't be many doors away.

At the end of his first day, he returned home, having sold nothing. Refusing to give up, he sat down to learn more about the products he was selling. Perhaps if I learned more about these Watkins products, he told himself, I could really believe in them and share that belief with others. Then they would buy them!

Hour after hour passed as he tried to memorize every item and price in the catalogs. What size boxes does the laundry detergent come in? Is the cinnamon really the freshest on the market? Is it cheaper and wiser to sell the large size? What's my commission? Based on the literature, Bill decided he could be proud of what he was selling. But it wasn't until Bill came to the sentence "Watkins, Inc., backs their products with a 100 percent money-back guarantee" that his enthusiasm really soared. The implications to Bill were huge. What a sales tactic! He pictured himself promising an unsure customer that if they weren't 100 percent satisfied with their order, they could get their money back. In other words, the customer wasn't risking anything.

He called the district manager the next day to verify that the company really would refund a customer's money if they weren't satisfied. The manager answered "Yes," unaware that Bill intended to use this guarantee to the fullest extent possible. If Watkins, Inc., was so sure customers would love their vanilla extract that they had the guarantee etched right onto the glass container, then surely this was a great product that was almost never returned. Theoretically, a customer could even use up to one-fourth of the bottle and still get a refund! If Watkins was that confident about their products, then Bill certainly should be. He decided to project that confidence and enthusiasm as part of his sales presentation. He could hardly wait to hit the streets. He knew he would make a sale.

Bill tells the story of his first sale as if it happened yesterday, when in fact it was more than four decades ago.

"I wasn't doing too well selling in that first territory until I came upon an apartment building. I had a good feeling about the place. Unfortunately, I couldn't get into the building. Every entrance was locked. I didn't know what to do, but I knew I had to get inside. Then I got an idea. I decided to hide just inside the porch behind a pillar. When someone came along to open the door, I would grab it before it shut and sneak in."

And Bill did exactly that. He started knocking on doors inside that building and finally made his first sale on the third floor. In complete honesty, he assured the lady that she would get her money back in full if she wasn't satisfied with the way the cleanser worked. "Okay," the lady said, "where do I sign?" Eventually Bill made quite a few new friends and customers in that building. Persistence finally paid off for Bill Porter. His mother would be ecstatic.

Unfortunately, Ernest Porter passed away in his sleep on September 8, 1962, one day before Bill's thirtieth birthday and only five months after Bill won his first sales award.

Father and son never took the time to talk about his success. Bill doesn't remember why their lives had drifted apart. Perhaps they were both too busy working. Bill would always struggle with his feelings about his father, always wondering if his job with Watkins satisfied the man who etched into Bill's brain the command "Get a job." Would Bill still hear those words if his father was alive today? Regardless, what mattered most then was that he now had a job and he was going to keep it. He also was going to excel at it beyond his father's wildest dreams. Bill was the man of the house now, and the sole provider for his mother.

It was sheer determination that landed Bill his job at Watkins, Inc. Eventually, he became the top-selling Watkins salesman in the entire Northwest, a position he continues to hold today.

Bill's amazing persistence is one of many character traits that admiring fans often mention in their numerous cards, letters, and e-mails. Readers report that they are better able to persevere through their own day-to-day and lifelong problems after they hear Bill's stories. The Brady family is no exception. Our fourteen-year-old daughter, Katrina, was diagnosed with PVNS (pigmented villa-nodular synovitis) in 1998. In layperson terms, this rare disease is essentially a reoccurring benign tumor within the knee joint, resulting in severe pain and limited mobility. Thankfully, PVNS is not life or limb threatening; the doctors have operated on her five times since the diagnosis to remove the tumor. We hope the last procedure will finally stop the growth, but many more surgeries may be in her future.

As you can imagine, Katrina's disease and physical handicap is at times devastating and incomprehensible to her. On the way home from the last operation, with her leg in a brace and crutches in the back seat, I glanced over to gauge her mental state, figuring that she would be completely depressed and in need of encouraging motherly words. To my surprise, she was looking out the window with a smile on her face. I remarked, "I'm glad to see you're handling this so well, honey." She replied, "I was just thinking of Bill."

Don't Take "No" for an Answer

According to the *Merriam-Webster Dictionary*, the word "no" is an act or instance of refusing or denying something. For instance, a customer's refusal to purchase goods or services from a salesperson is generally expressed via the word "no." For some reason or another, Bill Porter doesn't hear it that way. Bill hears the word "no" differently; he hears it to mean that the customer will be glad for Bill to return at a more convenient time or pleased to be shown another, more necessary product.

"No" is a powerful word used by children, parents, educators, and business associates. How one relates to it is shaped in early childhood, where many of us learned only the literal dictionary definition of the word. In adulthood, many of us still fear the word, and sometimes unhealthy or unstable relationships can be damaged or destroyed when a "no" is heard from someone close to us.

I learned from Bill Porter that when someone says "no" they are simply asking you to modify your proposal or change your delivery. I believe that Bill's attitude toward the word "no" and his ability not to focus on the "negative" are traits that many people admire in him.

Some have interpreted Bill's cerebral palsy as one gigantic "no" dished out by the heavens, but he never looked at it that way. I have to admit there was a time when a blemish on my face before a Saturday night dance felt like more of a handicap than Bill's cerebral palsy was to him his entire life. When he could have collected disability or at least taken a job that wasn't so mentally and physically demanding, Bill chose instead a profession — door-to-door sales — that challenged his so-called "handicap."

Bill's association with Watkins began in December 1961. Expecting the worst, the district manager gave Bill a territory in Portland that no one else wanted and where sales were almost nonexistent. The houses were run-down and many households were so strapped for cash that anything Bill had to offer for sale was considered a luxury.

"It was hard to sell there because many of the people weren't home," Bill recalls. "They were all working to make ends meet. There were times I felt like quitting but knew I couldn't."

Bill managed to eke a meager income out of this poverty-stricken area. However, he and his mother worried about Ernest's health and the possibility of a day when his father would no longer contribute to the family income. Bill knew it was time to pursue a more lucrative territory or get another job. He approached his district manager with an idea.

"What if I took the territory near my home, the one where I sold baskets for United Cerebral Palsy? What if I sold Watkins products there? I already have a client base." The manager told him the territory belonged to someone else. Bill was ready for that one.

"According to the research I've done, Watkins doesn't have a policy concerning territories." Bill was right. At the time, territories were loosely defined and assigned; salesmanship and performance weren't determining factors. Bill thought his track record should be taken into account, as well as his proximity and knowledge of the area. The manager's answer was a flat-out "No. The territory is taken."

This didn't quell Bill's need and desire for a better territory. He figured he simply had to present more compelling logic to the manager. A week later Bill approached him again.

"It wouldn't really be like I was stealing someone else's area. It would be more like I was getting my old territory back, like a reunion. You know it's the territory where I belong."

The manager said he needed a few weeks to think about it. Bill knew he had a foot in the door. Next time, he would close the deal.

At their next meeting, Bill flatly stated, "I'll sell more Watkins products than anyone in the history of Portland. I know I can do it. Just think of the money Watkins will make — and you, too — since you make commissions on what I do."

Reluctantly, the manager gave in to Bill's request. Bill told him he would never regret it. In fact, it only took three months in his new territory for Bill to become a member of the Watkins $1000 Club, an achievement for which he received an impressive certificate. Irene framed it herself and proudly displayed it on the wall. Two months later, Bill was featured in Watkins News. The following article appeared in the July 9, 1962 issue:

PORTER POSTS $1076 SALES MONTH, KEEPS PACE WITH TOP PORTLAND DEALERS

Bill Porter of North Portland, Oregon, showed during May that with the help of sales aids, a determined effort, and spending eight solid hours, five to six days per week, in face-to-face selling, profits come comparatively easy. A good indication of this was his $1076 total for the month and an impressive $340 for the short Memorial Day holiday week.

Since becoming a dealer in December 1961, he has consistently followed Company-suggested sales methods and has placed primary emphasis on the liberal use of Catalogs and Free Gifts. During the month of May he purchased five full cases of Catalogs and had a young boy strew them in his locality.

Due to a handicap, Porter is unable to drive a car and he therefore walks upwards of seventy blocks from his home to his locality in a six-day week. According to Distributors Ted and Isaac Marto, Porter's eight-hour day begins when he reaches his locality, not when he leaves home. Porter has

achieved his remarkable sales despite a physical handicap
and a speech impediment. Division Manager C. C. Hunter
says about Porter: "It's amazing that Porter can come forth
with such outstanding sales. It's no small wonder that he
puts other dealers to shame."

Irene Porter was immensely proud of Bill's achievements. She clipped the newsletter article and carried it in her purse. Bill still blushes when he tells the story of Irene bragging to friends and neighbors about the article, as if he'd been elected the president of Watkins.

Ernest and Bill never did discuss Bill's achievements, and to this day I sense that Bill still feels a little cheated; he wishes his dad had at least shook his hand or given him a pat on the back.

The accolades Bill received from corporate headquarters inspired him to work harder. The certificate and the news article were proof positive that Bill was a great salesman. He awoke every morning confident that he would sell more than the day before, and he carried this positive attitude throughout each day. The following statement from Bill is a good example of how he focuses on the positive, rather than the negative.

"If there were ten houses on a block, I would go to each one of them. It didn't matter if some families took better care of their yards or cars than others did. In each one lived a potential customer. If people in eight of the ten houses told me no, I wasn't discouraged because that meant two families bought from me. In three months when I covered that block again, I would go to all ten houses. Some salespeople would only go back to the houses they had successfully sold to. Not me. I knew that eventually people in each of those eight houses would buy from me, and many did! I knocked on the front door of every house in my territory about once every three months. Eventually, I built up to more than five hundred regular customers."

Everyday, Bill would knock on doors for eight hours, covering seven to ten miles on foot, rain or shine. He

 knocked at approximately one hundred homes per day, and if he was lucky, one in ten would buy something. Other days he might have as few as five orders at the end of his beat. If he was fortunate enough to get beyond the usual "Not interested," he knew he was on his way to a sale. If someone invited him in, it was a done deal for sure.

Mrs. Brown is now a regular client of Bill's, but for years she resisted. There was a time she told Bill to never come back because there wasn't a chance in heaven that she would order anything in his catalog. Mrs. Brown was flabbergasted when he would show up every three months just to make sure she wasn't running short of something like cinnamon or laundry soap. One day Mrs. Brown reluctantly let Bill into her house. His timing happened to be perfect because he discovered that she was running low on vanilla and it was just before Thanksgiving. She remembers, "Bill had it all figured out. He wouldn't leave until I bought something. He'd just keep showing me products until I saw something I really needed."

Bill has a special fondness for Mrs. Brown. "Out of my five hundred steady customers," he says, "about forty are people who told me they didn't want anything and to never come back. Today, they are some of my best customers! Mrs. Brown was one of those forty."

Bill has the memory of an elephant when it comes to remembering when his customers are out of essentials. He knows, for example, when Mrs. Brown's bottle of window cleaner is starting to suck air. One customer relates that when Bill visited her in May he was set to write her up for a box of detergent. She politely explained that the family would be gone for three months on vacation, camping, and visiting relatives. They would use laundromats and wouldn't need detergent until they got back. She asked Bill when he would be back in her neighborhood and expected a very approximate answer such as "sometime in the fall."

"I'll be back the morning of August nineteenth," Bill replied. Exactly three months later to the day, Bill appeared on her doorstep, order book in hand, ready to write up the detergent. She can't say she was too surprised, since Bill managed to sell her some insect repellent before she left on vacation!

Over the many years I delivered products for Bill, I came across a few customers who would pull me aside and ask for help. They had placed orders with Bill on the spur of the moment because they liked his enthusiasm and upbeat attitude, but they later realized that they didn't need them. They just didn't know how to say "no" to Bill, and when they did he didn't seem to hear them; he just kept showing them new Watkins products. Their cupboards were filled with jars and boxes of unopened spices, pasta, and bagel mixes. Bill could sell soup mixes to people who ate every meal out and meat tenderizers to vegetarians. I'd just shrug my shoulders, wish them luck, and say, "See you next time."

After many years of watching and learning from the pro, I am finally able to proclaim that I have learned to adopt and institute Bill's attitude towards negativity. Numerous times, at critical junctures in my life, I have said to myself, "If Bill Porter refuses to take 'no' for an answer, why should Shelly Brady?" And like magic, it worked! Since I started adopting this new attitude, my personal and professional life has blossomed. Doors to opportunity that were always shut have suddenly swung open. The following story illustrates just such a door opening.

Bill and I have spent the last few years traveling and sharing his story with companies all over the world. Audience response has been terrific, and requests for our services have been phenomenal. However, our enterprise hit some rocky roads during its start-up. When businesses first started calling to book us, Bill said, "No! No way!" As far as he was concerned, he was a salesman, not a public speaker.

So in the finest Bill Porter style, I replied, "Wait a minute, Bill. This is right up my alley. You're forgetting that I majored in theatre. I love the stage. Besides, the publicity might help sales." Bill suddenly grew quiet; he may very well have been crunching numbers. A few moments later Bill agreed to participate in at least one speaking engagement. Many more followed, of course.

Our enterprise has been a dream come true for me: following my passion, speaking and inspiring others. I am constantly amazed by how many hearts are touched by Bill's story. Being a bit of a showman himself, Bill loves the attention but is more impressed

with how his sales of Watkins products have skyrocketed since becoming a celebrity.

The year 2000 was unbelievably busy for Bill and me. The previous year had been filled with presentations, writing the first draft of this book, interviews, and a television movie deal. Bill continued to service his door-to-door Watkins accounts even though he could now afford to live off his speaking income. I somehow managed to keep my family life in order despite flying off to speaking appointments and meeting with movie producers, all the while toting child number six in my belly. When an agency specializing in booking speakers approached with a desire to represent us, I was ecstatic. Up to this time, I'd been managing all aspects of our tours: the airline flights, the hotel reservations, and the presentation itself. However, signing with a professional agency has its pluses and minuses. Spontaneity and improvisation had to be kept to a minimum. When the agency booked, we had to be willing, ready, and able. We polished our presentation and included video clips. Bill and Shelly were going Hollywood!

Our agent scheduled a presentation with Williams Communications in January of 2000. Since I would be

 eight-and-a-half months pregnant at the time, my husband, John, agreed to accompany Bill on the trip. I videotaped my portion of the presentation and our agent was satisfied that all would go well. However, just days before Bill and my husband were to fly to Orlando, Florida, Bill complained of not feeling well and that he was having breathing difficulties. I thought his complaints were psychosomatic because I wouldn't be by his side. Our relationship with the speaking bureau appeared to be ending before it began. What's a mother to do? The five previous pregnancies were never more than three days early, so the odds were that I would be home well before labor began. And so against the doctor's orders and airline policy, I decided to join Bill and make the trip to Orlando. But this didn't pacify him; now he was worried about my health as well.

Two days before we were scheduled to fly out, Bill

decided he simply wasn't feeling good enough to make the trip. I felt in my heart that Bill was physically okay. Yes, he suffered from acid reflux due to pain medications he'd taken after an accident three years before. The doctors did manage to get the acid reflux under control, but due to his cerebral palsy some of the acid had dripped into his lungs, scarring them, and he had to use an inhaler twice a day. Other than an occasional episode when he couldn't catch his breath for a few moments, he got along fine, running his errands, selling, and traveling. I begged and pleaded with Bill to try and make the trip. He simply refused.

My world seemed to come to an end that night. I couldn't sleep, one minute sobbing into my pillow about my outcast state, the next minute stoically facing the reality that my life as a speaker was over. On the one hand I was sad because Bill's inspiring story wouldn't reach an audience that wanted to hear it, and on the other I was selfishly depressed because my own dreams were going down the drain. I loved the stage, the lights, the cameras, and the applause.

The next morning I decided out of desperation to try the Bill Porter don't-take-no-for-an-answer approach to a problem. I phoned our representative at the agency to sell them on a novel approach to the dilemma. What if I flew to Orlando without Bill and, using the latest audio-video technologies, he appeared on screen via satellite feed, much like at the Academy Award Ceremonies when the winner is unable to attend? It all made perfect sense to me because when we signed with the agency we talked about the future and how the day would come when Bill would no longer be up to traveling and speaking. Things would simply get speeded up, that's all! However, our agent had hoped to establish Bill and I as speakers together for at least a year or two before I appeared alone. He certainly didn't anticipate Bill's inability to fulfill his commitment with one of the agency's best clients.

I persisted and explained to our agent that we had little to lose at this point. If I went "belly-up" (pun intended) on stage and the clients wanted their money back, so be it. We'd survive. Bill still had Watkins products to sell and I had my family. The conversation ended with an "I'll get back to you."

Within an hour our agent phoned and asked how soon I could pack my bags — I was on my way to Disney World (and hoping that child number six would wait until I got back). The presentation went well with me alone on stage and Bill live in the background on large screen television via satellite. Williams Communications was so pleased they invited us to speak again two months later in Las Vegas (this time with baby in tow). This invitation came with full knowledge that Bill might not be able to make it in person. As it turns out, Bill's health took a turn for the better, and we continued with our scheduled speaking engagements for the next few months. One of the conference planners was so touched by Bill's story that she approached him with the idea of being the spokesperson for Williams Communications. Bill was flattered, but the timing was wrong and the deal never panned out. He found it ironic, though, that he was once fired for not communicating well over the telephone, and now here he was being considered for the position of spokesman for a major communications company.

Bill knew his traveling days would be over sooner than I wanted them to be. As romantic as life on the road sounds, it takes a toll on the body and the spirit. Dorothy of *The Wizard of Oz* was right when she said, "There's no place like home." Airports, ground transportation, hotels, and restaurants all take their toll. They are especially tough on a person as well organized as Bill; his success is based on a well-orchestrated daily routine.

On another much-anticipated trip, Bill reluctantly told me he couldn't come along, and I knew he was really suffering. Bill's doctors even recommended that he take some time at home to regain his full health.

The situation was very distressing to our client. Many of the conventioneers had bought tickets in anticipation of meeting the main feature, Mr. Bill Porter. The agency's reputation was also on the line; contractually, they had agreed that Bill would appear in person at the convention. Bill's name was in bold-faced type on the program. Attendees were flying from all over the country to see and hear Bill Porter, not Shelly Brady.

When our agent called the person in charge to break the bad news about Bill's health, offering me as a consolation prize, the door slammed shut. The promoters of this convention were not as flexible as Williams Communications. The answer was a resounding "No. No Shelly without Bill." My life as a speaker once again appeared to be over.

In another one of those Bill Porter moments, I got an

idea. I called the convention organizers directly and told them I was confident I could share Bill's story myself with Bill possibly linked via satellite or telephone. I assured them I did it previously and it was very well received. I told them I would personally lay my speaking fee on the table. They could pay me whatever they felt my presentation was worth, even if it meant I'd get nothing. I was confident they had to accept my offer. I felt like Bill Porter telling a Watkins customer, "Satisfaction guaranteed or your money back." On top of that, I wasn't about to take "no" for an answer.

The chief organizer of the convention agreed to consider my offer and promised to get back to me. My agent was on pins and needles, and probably searching for new clients. An hour later the phone rang. Yes, the company would take me up on my offer. I would attend and speak in person with Bill connected via telephone. They would determine our speaking fee once it was over and the audience response was evaluated. I called my husband at work to tell him I was leaving town the next day.

"I'm not surprised," he remarked. "Nobody says no to you, dear."

Or Bill Porter, I thought. Two weeks later, a check arrived for the full speaking fee.

CHAPTER 6

Know Your Limits and Reach Beyond Them

At the 1996 Watkins International Convention in New Orleans, Bill Porter received a standing ovation when he closed the meeting by telling the audience, "Go out there and do the best job you can." The theme of the convention was "Achieving Goals," and the meetings and speeches promoted the belief that seemingly impossible goals can be realized by assessing one's limitations and reaching beyond them. Bill is living proof of that ideal.

Some of us are lucky enough to know exactly what our goals are, which, according to Bill, means the battle is half won. He believes great experiences and memories line the pathway leading towards the achievement of goals. Once you know in your heart your goal is the right one, even small steps toward achieving it will give you a sense of accomplishment. Bill found his calling — sales — early on and followed that path no matter how steep the hills or deep the valleys. He can recount endless stories about the ups and downs of his journey towards his goal of becoming a first class salesman.

Bill's attitude about setting and achieving goals can be traced to his youth when he developed a passion for sports. He smiles broadly when he talks about listening to baseball games with his parents, when they would all sit around the dining table next to a huge radio. That was before the days of television, when active imaginations were necessary to visualize all the action.

Bill still cherishes his scrapbook of autographed pictures of the New York Yankees. (He wrote the team manager asking for an autographed baseball and received photos instead.) Bill and his folks followed all professional sports, and visitors to the Porter household knew a lively discussion about the pros and cons of various teams and the players was inevitable. Many nights before Bill went to sleep, he imagined himself playing sports. He dreamed of hitting a grand slam or throwing the winning touchdown. Sadly, the fact that he had cerebral palsy always snapped him back to the reality that his physical limitations prevented him from even joining the neighborhood boys at the local sandlot.

When Bill entered high school, he found a way to circumvent his condition and enjoy sports as much as other children. He asked the coach if he could be the team's water boy, and the coach gladly obliged because nobody else wanted the task. At every game, Bill passed out towels and filled water cups for the active players, but he didn't stop there; he got the idea of making himself the official keeper of team statistics. "The day before the game," he remembers, "I'd type all the players' names in a column and the different plays across the top. I'd bring my paper and pencil to the game and mark each play by the appropriate player. Each night after the game, I would

LINCOLN HIGH SCHOOL
Portland, Oregon
Athletic Award
This is to Certify that

_____
BILL PORTER
has been awarded a

FIRST YEAR MANAGER'S *letter in* ____VARSITY BASEBALL____
for the season of ____1953-54____

stay up half the night typing up the stats to give to the coach the next day."

Later, Bill worked as a sports writer for the Lincoln High newspaper. In his column, he wrote about the highlights of the game, followed by the complete statistics. His column was titled "Porter's Tips." His contributions to sports at Lincoln High School were much appreciated, and he was awarded with a letter jacket at the senior banquet. Today, the jacket is one of his most prized possessions and it still hangs in his closet, ready to be modeled by Bill for anyone who asks about it. The 1954 yearbook for Lincoln High School lists Bill Porter as the "most likely to become a sportswriter for the *New York Times*." Bill successfully accomplished his goal of participating in sports by knowing his limitations and reaching beyond them. He cherishes his sports memories at Lincoln High School as much as any varsity quarterback.

In the 1980s, Bill and I both learned a sobering lesson

about the limited time one has here on this earth when his mother, Irene, exhibited early signs of Alzheimer's disease. Bill remembers the moment clearly:

"It started out of the blue. One day I was getting ready to go to work and my mother started complaining. She hadn't been feeling well and she said I was a terrible son for going off and leaving her alone. I didn't know what to do. I knew I had to go to work. I had to pay the bills. She would be fine for a few days and then it would start all over again. Mother would cry when I left in the mornings and when I got home she wouldn't speak to me for a couple of hours."

It was the most excruciatingly painful experience in Bill's life. His heroine and biggest supporter seemed to be turning against him. He knew in his heart that it wasn't really his mother talking, but some illness he didn't understand. Still, it took every ounce of his will power to walk out the door each morning, never knowing if his mother would greet him with silence or tears when he returned.

After learning from the family doctor that Irene was stricken with Alzheimer's, he hired a neighbor to assist her while he was at work. Her condition worsened over the next few months and before long she required twenty-four-hour care. Bill was forced to place her in a foster home where he hoped the homey environment would comfort her, but he quickly realized she wasn't getting the attention she needed, and he moved her to a nursing home with more intensive care.

I began working for Bill regularly after I returned from college, shortly before he placed Irene in the nursing home.

I watched him faithfully visit her over the remaining years of her life. Every Tuesday and Thursday evening after work, Bill would take the bus to Saint Joseph's Nursing Home. Since he worked long days, he often didn't arrive until after regular visiting hours were over. The nurses always nodded him in, as they appreciated the love and devotion he had for his mother. Every Sunday after church, Bill spent the entire afternoon with her. This schedule never changed, even when her condition worsened to the point where she didn't even recognize him.

As our relationship evolved from employer/employee to friendship, Bill turned to my family and me for comfort and support. We opened up our personal lives to each other. I usually talked about how busy I was with my two toddlers, and he invariably talked about Irene and her condition. Progressively, his reports grew worse and worse, from "a little better" to "okay" to "not so well." I sensed his mother's time here on earth was nearing an end.

He asked me if I would like to visit her, but unfortunately I didn't go right away; I was so busy with my own affairs: selling our house, shopping for a new one, volunteering at the church, and participating at a child care cooperative. Time slipped away, and Bill, like a bird on my shoulder, periodically asked, "Shelly, do you think you could come with me sometime soon to visit my mother?" I really wanted to go with him and promised I would check my calendar. Things were so hectic. The children needed me. The church needed me. I was experiencing severe headaches that the doctor told me were due to my being pregnant. Life was so busy, with home shopping and doctor visits and those excruciating headaches.

Through it all, I'd hear the occasional "Shelly, please come with me to visit my mother."

"Soon," I promised. "How about one week from today? We're right in the middle of selling our house."

Exactly one week later, while I was getting ready to deliver Watkins Products, I started spotting blood. Frantic, I phoned the doctor's office for advice, and the nurse assured me, "There is nothing to worry about. Bleeding is quite common. Everything will be fine."

I asked her if I should go to bed or stay off my feet. She told me not to change my routine. If I were going to miscarry, I would miscarry. There was nothing I could do to change it. With great trepidation, I completed packing the orders for Bill.

Later that evening at Bill's house, I sensed that something was seriously wrong with me and decided to postpone our date to visit his mother until I felt better. "Minor female discomfort" was all I said, as I didn't want to upset him with the details of my difficult pregnancy. He was very prone to doting over me, and he had enough on his mind between his mother and his business.

My children spent the day with grandma while I stoically delivered the customers' Watkins products. I was so confident in my ability to deal with the pregnancy that I encouraged my husband to spend the weekend with his brothers in

Seattle celebrating multiple birthdays. I promised to call if things got worse.

Sunday morning, I found myself in bed cramping, bleeding, and crying as I waited for John, my husband, to make the three-hour drive home from Seattle. We went immediately to the hospital emergency room, where the doctor tried to locate the baby's heartbeat. There was none! I lay in excruciating pain for hours, pleading for painkillers and verbally attacking every nurse who entered my room.

"I don't do labor," I demanded. "I get epidurals. I don't do this when I am pregnant. Why do I have to do it now?"

Finally, I was wheeled to the ultrasound room where a nurse matter-of-factly informed me that the fetus was dead. Suddenly I felt a gush and the attendant bluntly exclaimed, "Oh, here it is. You've miscarried. It's all over." I sat up to see. She pushed me back down and said, "You don't want to see this."

As she exited the room with my baby wrapped in a towel, she turned and said, "The doctor will be in shortly to perform a D and C, which is a procedure to clean out your insides." (Those really were her exact words!)

There were flowers, cards, meals brought in, and lots of hugs, but no baby. Thanks to two healthy children and a loving husband my life went on. We explained to the children that the baby in mommy's tummy got sick, died, and went to heaven.

Before I knew it, two months went by, and we were at last moved into our much-needed larger home. Life was just beginning to settle down when I heard those familiar words: "Shelly, will you come with me to see my mother?" I was finally able to spend an evening with Bill and his mother.

It was a warm August evening when I drove with Bill to Saint Joseph's Nursing Home. He talked nonstop about his mother: how she had changed, how things used to be, how I wouldn't recognize her, and how long it had been since she recognized him. He spoke of her sense of humor, how she loved looking her best, and how stubborn she could be. Bill said the doctors didn't think she would live much longer. He couldn't imagine life without her. In a sense, with her Alzheimer's disease so advanced, she was already gone.

We arrived at Saint Joseph's and Bill led the way to his mother's room. Our visit was brief; a shriveled shell of a  woman lay in bed and stared vacantly at the curtain separating her from her roommate. Her mouth quivered slightly, releasing a senseless, soft muttering. Bill moved close to her, and leaning over he whispered, "Mother, there's someone I want you to see. Do you remember Shelly? Mother? Mother?" Her eyes remained vacant. There was no sign of recognition. She just lay there, rocking, moaning, and pulling at her fingers. The look in Bill's eyes broke my heart. I think my presence must have brought the reality of her condition into perspective for Bill. He fidgeted, looked at his watch, and said, "She's not herself. We should go."

I asked Bill if we could stay for a few more minutes. He looked nervous and upset but agreed. I approached Irene and said, "Mrs. Porter, it's me Shelly. I'm Bill's friend. I work for him."

I gently placed my hand on her forehead and brushed her thin gray hair away from her face. I took her hand in mine, and she stopped rocking. "That's a pretty good kid you have there. He turned out all right. He can be a tough boss, though."

Bill smiled at that. Then I leaned over and whispered in her ear. "Don't worry about Bill. He's going to be just fine. He's a part of my family now, and we'll keep an eye on him for you." I gave her a soft kiss on the forehead and then stepped back so Bill could say his good-bye.

The drive home was mostly quiet and subdued; we both knew her death was not far away. Bill felt a need to apologize. "I'm so sorry. That just wasn't my mother. She's changed so much in the past few months. I wish you could have seen her sooner." Tears came to my eyes and I said, "So do I Bill, so do I. I'm so sorry."

One week later Bill called me; I could barely understand him through the sobbing. "My mother... the doctor called ...it's my mom...she's dying...can you come now? Will you come with me?"

"I'm on my way," I said.

She was gone by the time we got there. Her body remained atop the bed, eyes open, more vacant than before, cheeks sunken in, and her mouth open as if she tried to utter some last words. Her hair was a disheveled mess and her arthritic hands were clenched. It was a very discomforting sight, and Bill could hardly stand to see her like that. Moving to her bedside, he fell across her, sobbing, "Mother, oh mother."

I felt so awkward being there, just watching, like an intruder standing in the shadows. Bill was draped over her body, tears streaming down his face. I wanted to leave him alone with her, but I couldn't just walk away; he might need me at any moment. I placed my hand on his shoulder to let him know he wasn't alone in this world.

After a few more minutes he was ready to go. During the drive home, Bill was silent except for an occasional stifled sob. I can't remember the exact words of comfort I offered, but they

seemed to help as his sobs became fewer and farther between.

The next day the priest, the nursing facility, and the funeral home helped Bill arrange the funeral. Five days later I stood by Bill's side at the funeral parlor with Irene in a casket for final viewing, but Bill wouldn't approach her. I left him with friends while I walked to the casket. She was wearing a beautiful dress Bill had selected for her. Her hair was neatly styled and the color in her face was restored with makeup. She looked at peace, as if she were only napping — nothing like the way I saw her only five nights before. I knew Bill needed to see her like this before the burial.

I approached him and said, "You really should see your

mother." He said, "No, Shelly, I can't. I don't want to remember her like this." I pressed further. "I think it would be a good thing for you to say good-bye one last time." I knew that if Bill viewed her now it would help erase the image of her in that hospital room.

He kept saying "No" and I, in turn, gently persisted. "Bill, trust me. She looks so young and beautiful. Come with me. Come say good-bye." He finally went limp, and I took his hand and led him to the casket. He was amazed how beautiful she looked. "That's how I remember her. Isn't she beautiful? Thank you, Shelly." I watched as he caressed her hands and touched her cheek. He then leaned over and whispered in her ear, "Good-bye."

Bill made it through his mother's death, resumed his daily routine, and went on to become the role model he is today. The Brady family carried on, too; our third daughter, Teressa Amy Nicole, was born May 2, 1990. I learned from Bill that

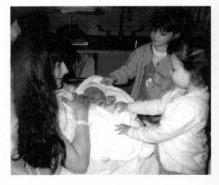

death need not devastate the living. The last thing Irene would have wanted was for Bill to be incapacitated by her death. Instead, her memory continued to motivate and influence Bill's life as he went on to become a great salesman and an inspiration to many. Whenever Bill receives acknowledgement for his achievements, he always humbly replies, "My mother would be so proud."

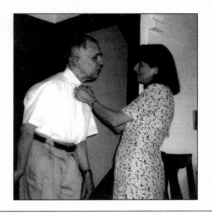

Be a Team Player

At first glance, watching Bill Porter trek up the steep side-walks and driveways of his West Portland territory, one sees a solitary man going it alone against the elements. Often it's only Bill and the mailman out there in the rain, sleet, or snow. The mailman is supported by the U.S. Postal Service with its fleet of airplanes, trucks, clerks, and mail sorters; Bill isn't so lucky. Although Watkins, Inc., provides Bill with some support, he is essentially an independent representative who can't count on a substitute to fill in for him when he's sick or when it's raining and the wind is blowing sideways. Over the years, however, Bill has assembled his own team of support personnel that allow him to perform his job as efficiently as the mail carrier (some say more efficiently) in spite of his physical handicaps.

I've known and worked for Bill for more than twenty

years and was surprised and a little embarrassed to learn from Tom Hallman's November 1995 feature article in the *Oregonian* that there are members of his team I knew nothing about. Hallman followed Bill on foot to learn exactly how a person with cerebral palsy could accomplish the phenomenal feats that Bill does on a daily basis. He learned the extensive list of players on Bill's team, carefully chosen by Bill over the years, as necessity and situations dictated.

When Irene became ill and was placed in a nursing home, Bill was alone for the first time in his life. He'd never shopped for groceries, prepared meals, or done his own laundry. Irene handled those things while Bill was busy doing what he does best — selling. It didn't take more than a few days for Bill to realize he didn't have the time or physical ability to actually shop, cook, and clean if he intended to service his accounts properly. He quickly put out the word to friends, neighbors, and the congregation at his church that he was hiring for various tasks. Two people from church answered his call. Bill needed one of them to shop, clean the house, and wash his clothes, and the other to keep his yard presentable. Both offered to perform these duties for free. This sounded too much like charity to Bill; he has always insisted on paying people the going wage. I believe that one reason Bill prefers to pay people for their services is because he can then expect a higher level of job performance from everyone he hires.

Bill wasn't a novice employer. Since 1961 he has employed people, including myself, to deliver Watkins products. My association with him began in 1980 when I answered an ad he posted on the Grant High School Job Board. In 1987, I took on other duties for Bill, including housecleaning, laundry, and grocery shopping.

Occasionally, before church or social gatherings, I would button Bill's cuffs or tie his shoelaces for him, never questioning how these tasks were performed when I wasn't around. I must have presumed he had better control of his fingers back then, or someone else magically appeared every day to help him out. Tom Hallman found the latter to be closer to the truth. He followed Bill one morning to the Vintage Plaza Hotel in downtown Portland, where years before Bill had approached the manager to ask for assistance with his buttons and tie. Bill tells the story this way:

"The day after I had my mother placed in a foster home, I didn't know what I'd do. She was always there for me. She would button my cuffs and collar and put on my tie. I thought about it for a while and then I got an idea. The bus stop downtown where I made my transfer to the West Hills bus was near the Vintage Plaza Hotel. I would carry my tie in my briefcase and ask the manager there if the bellhops could help me."

The manager, Craig Thompson, was happy to accommodate Bill. Every week, Monday through Friday, just after 8:00 A.M., Bill would arrive in the lobby of the hotel, cuffs unbuttoned and tie stashed in his briefcase. Guests and employees came and went but Bill was always there. If it was a busy morning, Bill would patiently wait out of the way until one of the bellhops could assist him. He never waited long, though; they always tried to help him as quickly as they could because they knew he had a full day ahead of him. The employees of the hotel had a good rapport with Bill, too. They all felt they were essentially in the same line of work — pleasing their customers. Bill came to know them all personally; he learned about their birthdays, college applications, marriages, and children.

When Craig Thompson transferred to the Fifth Avenue Suites Hotel a few blocks away, Bill made the switch as well. Craig was delighted to have a familiar face greet him each morning, and Bill quickly made new friends with the staff there. I once asked Bill if it bothered him that he had to ask for help with his tie and buttons.

"It's something I have to do," he replied. "It doesn't bother me at all. The people at the hotel are my friends and they like to help me. I don't look at myself as different from any other person just because I need a little help. It's just part of my daily routine."

The bellhops refused payment for this small service — not even a tip — and, remarkably, Bill accepted the arrangement based on friendship.

After talking with Bill about his dependence on others to complete his dressing, I wondered if under the same circumstances I would have had the courage to ask others for help. I quickly realized that we all need help, we all lack skill of some sort or another. It's just that most of our inabilities aren't so visually evident as Bill's; they may be psychological rather than physical, and, often, we create them ourselves. And, as we all know, some of our self-imposed mental disabilities can be more difficult to overcome than physical ones. All Bill Porter needs is someone to button his cuffs and clip his tie; it's the rest of us who need attitude adjustments, R&R, and pep talks. In my clearest moments, I am able to see Bill Porter as he sees himself and truly say "What disability?"

When *Oregonian* journalist Tom Hallman approached Bill about writing an article about him, Bill wondered why anyone would want to read about his life. Several years later, he still wonders what all the fuss is about. He's amazed at the letters, gifts, awards, and media attention. It moves him deeply to be told he is a role model, a hero. With humble gratitude he has accepted gifts of money for future medical expenses and retirement. He is touched that businesses, schools, and churches want to hear his story. For example,

after hearing Bill and I speak, one company (Primerica Financial Services) sent Bill and the entire Brady family to Disneyland. When asked to comment on all that's happened, he simply responds, "My mother would be so proud. Sales have been very good. And, oh yeah, I got to ride Splash Mountain."

Bill simply doesn't have a clue about the millions of lives he has touched. After the *Oregonian* article, Bill's story was shared in several magazines and news shows. Eventually, ABC's *20/20* got wind of the story. After coming to Portland to film and interview Bill, ABC aired Bill's story, "A Moving Journey," on December 12, 1997. It received the largest viewer response in the history of the program. Thousands of readers faxed, phoned, e-mailed, and wrote, saying how inspired they were by Bill Porter's story.

Over the more than twenty years I've been on Bill's team, many people have told me that I'm an angel for delivering Watkins products for him. I immediately correct them.

"I'm no angel. Bill pays me! I work for him. He's my boss!"

The first time Bill and I shared his story at a business meeting, I tried to explain our employee/employer relationship. Bill jumped right in. "Shelly's an angel." A good-natured argument took place as we went back and forth.

"I'm not an angel, Bill. I work for you," I would say.

Bill, normally quiet, responded with "I couldn't get along without Shelly." I shot right back, "Now that's a bunch of baloney, Bill. You got along for years without me, and if you hadn't hired me in 1980, you would have hired someone else."

Bill replied, "But I did hire you, Shelly. And you are an angel."

I managed to get in the last word. "All right, Bill, that's enough. These people didn't pay good money to bring us all this way to stand here and argue."

At the conclusion of a recent presentation to Callaway Golf in San Diego, I asked Bill if he had any words for the group. Bill replied, "Don't think about your handicaps or problems, think about the things you do have. And then be the best that you can be. That's what I try to do. And when I was too busy or unable to do something myself, I hired someone. I couldn't have sold all those products all these years without help from Shelly and many others. If my story could even touch maybe eleven lives, I would be so glad to have helped those people."

Of course, everyone who heard Bill speak that evening knew that his story has inspired thousands. Since Tom Hallman's article in the *Oregonian* and the *20/20* feature story, Bill's life and mine have been filled with appointments, travel, and speeches. It has been exciting and rewarding beyond my wildest dreams. However, since I am allotted only twenty-four hours per day, I soon felt the quality of my domestic life was in danger of being compromised. How was I going to maintain a successful business life and a healthy and happy family life? (Choosing to have six children didn't make the situation any easier.) In other words, how was I going to have my cake and eat it too? I took a cue from Bill Porter. I discovered I was surrounded by a trusted team of family, friends, and employees to help with my "handicap" of too many high goals and aspirations.

When Bill and I first began traveling to speaking engagements, I haphazardly enlisted the aid of my husband and various babysitters to hold down the fort while I was gone. I felt guilty about leaving the children to my loving husband whose hopes of a round of golf were now completely dashed. For awhile I would call home hourly to make sure everyone was fine. Did you change the diapers? What were your grades on your report card? I love you! See you in two days.

My self-esteem was never higher. My dream of standing on stage with an important message — the message of Bill Porter — was being fulfilled. My heart soared when the audience applauded. I was doing something important and fulfilling. At the same time, I was so worried about my family's well-being that by the time I off-loaded at the Portland International Airport, any good feelings that came from my speeches with Bill were dissipated by my sense of guilt for having left in the first place. If only I could merge my two worlds into one, but it was inconceivable to think that my family would be waiting in the green room after every presentation.

I had a mental handicap that was preventing me from enjoying what should be the happiest days of my life. I was brought up to think that I, the family matriarch, had to do everything myself. Finally, I gave in to a suggestion from Bill. He said, "Do what I did. Hire someone." And I did just that; I hired an occasional housekeeper. Surprisingly, I didn't feel less of a wife or mother for not doing all the household chores myself (not to mention the house is cleaner than ever).

When the requests for presentations by Bill and I reached four per month, I could no longer keep up with the paperwork, the travel arrangements, the billing, and the presentations themselves. I needed another member on my team to handle our bookings in a calm and professional manner. I then learned from a fellow speaker that there are agents who specialize in handling speakers such as Bill and I. They ensure that you are compensated fairly and that all arrangements are in order. Bill and I would then be able to concentrate on putting on a good show. The commission charged is more than made up for by the pressures the agency alleviates.

And so with the aid of family, friends, and a few employees, I am better able to appreciate the time I spend with my family, while the joy I get from traveling to share Bill's story lasts until our next adventure. From Bill, I learned to accept the help of others without feeling less of a person. I also learned that others are just as capable as I am of doing many tasks that I thought only I could do perfectly.

If It Isn't Broken, Don't Fix It

There is a fine line between disciplined persistence and plain old stubbornness. Bill walks that line every day of his life. Once he finds a routine that works, he sticks to it like glue.

For more than thirty years, Bill has followed a daily regimen like clockwork: up at 4:45, get dressed, eat breakfast, read the paper, listen to the weather report on the radio, have his mother help him with his tie and buttons, collect his briefcase, don his coat and hat, and head out the door to catch the 7:20 bus to downtown. Bill then walks three blocks to transfer to the number 10 bus, which takes him to his sales territory, the West Hills of Portland, arriving there at approximately 8:30.

Once in his sales district, he punches a mental time clock and doesn't consider punching out until at least an eight-hour day has been accomplished. All day long Bill walks up and down steep hills, knocking on doors and ringing doorbells; taking a break isn't even considered. But no matter where he is on his route, he stops for lunch at 1:30 P.M. sharp. In the past he liked to be near Saint Thomas More Church for lunch, where he would sit on a bench in the courtyard of the church and eat the lunch that Irene prepared for him. The priests and church secretaries could usually tell what time it was by Bill's arrival and departure. Sometimes Father Dernbach would sit and visit with him for awhile. When his pocket watch read 2:30, it was time to hit the pavement again.

Bill used to call it quits around 6:30, but as the years passed, more women joined the work force and he found fewer people at home during the day. Consequently, his workday stretched into the evening in order to catch customers arriving home from work. Most evenings it would be after 8:30 when he knocked on his last door. When Bill returned home, he'd orchestrate his evening hours as fastidiously as he choreographed his daylight hours. First, he sat in his easy chair, kicked off his shoes, and looked over his orders while his mother prepared dinner. Irene loved hearing every detail of Bill's day: who placed an order, who didn't and why, even if the knots on his shoelaces lasted all day. During dinner he'd usually listen to a radio talk show or sports event. Finally, he'd soak in a hot bath to try to get the kinks out of his back and sore muscles before climbing into bed by 11:00.

When his mother was no longer in their home to help Bill put the finishing touches on his sales attire, he added two stops to his morning ritual. First he'd stop at the shoeshine shop where he'd have his shoes shined and laces tightened, and then on to the Fifth Avenue Suites for help with his buttons and tie. In the evenings, Bill would turn the radio on for company and put two frozen TV dinners in the oven. When special errands had to be run, such as a haircut or shopping, Bill worked longer days to justify the time off.

When I started working for him as a teenager, I learned quickly that Bill likes things the way they are. I wasn't to move his furniture around or reorganize his knick-knacks. Once, while cleaning Bill's house, I folded and hung his bath towels the wrong way; he called me on the phone asking me if I was feeling all right. I said I felt fine. He was worried I might be ill because I had put the towels out improperly. I apologized and never got it wrong again!

When Watkins began encouraging sales representatives to consider multi-level marketing strategies, Bill wasn't interested; it didn't fit his style of selling. He thought it was fine that more than eighty thousand Watkins distributors built their businesses in that manner, but at that time Bill didn't want to spend his time and energy directing a "down-line." ("Down-line" refers to the customers and other sales people who work with a salesperson in a network.)

Years ago, Bill didn't have an answering machine, a VCR, a microwave, cable television, or a cordless phone. He still wouldn't if well-wishers hadn't given him all those things as gifts. Before they arrived on his front doorstep, I clearly remember Bill's outspokenness about modern gadgets.

"What use is an answering machine? I've gotten along for half a century just fine without owning one. If someone wants to reach me when I'm out, they'll keep trying if it's important enough. Why would I want to tie myself to a machine that makes me feel obligated to get back to someone I might not have wanted to talk to in the first place? Unless, of course, someone is calling to buy something from me."

Those calls are pretty rare because he stays on top of his customers' needs.

The VCR is still a mystery to Bill. It comes in handy when friends want to view the videotape of his appearance on ABC's *20/20,* a recent speaking engagement, or an awards ceremony. But he usually asks the guest to operate the VCR. Bill and I still chuckle about the time he complained that the VCR wasn't working; he told me he stuck in a tape and nothing happened. Thank goodness nothing happened — he'd inserted a cassette tape!

I was excited when Bill received a microwave as a gift. I thought it would cut down on food preparation time and ensure that he ate better, but he refused to touch it for three weeks. He spent another two weeks experimenting with opening and closing it. Finally, after many practice sessions, Bill felt comfortable warming one of his frozen dinners in the microwave, but since he eats two frozen dinners at his evening meal he still uses his conventional oven for one of them. I showed him how two dinners would fit in the microwave, but no amount of logic or coaxing convinced him to prepare his meals this way. There is something about the anticipation Bill feels while waiting the thirty to forty minutes it takes for a TV dinner to warm in the oven. It gives him time to sit down, take off his shoes, read the paper, and relax while the aroma of dinner fills the air. Perhaps it reminds him of the good old days when Irene made home-cooked meals.

Cable television was one of Bill's favorite gifts. Always an avid sports fan, he was now able to watch the Portland Trailblazers on Blazer Cable. Other than sports broadcasts, though, Bill rarely watches television. In fact, he prefers to watch games with the television volume turned down and the radio blaring. Having been a sports journalist in high school, Bill relates to the sports announcer whose goal is to paint a picture in the listener's mind.

The cordless phone is one modern gadget Bill adapted to immediately. Before this handy invention, Bill used to spend hours each month typing me a grocery list so I could do his shopping. Now, he walks around the kitchen, opens cupboards, and recites his needs to me via the cordless phone. This saves him time and ensures that he doesn't forget necessary items as he opens cupboard after cupboard. Once Bill was especially excited because he was calling me from his backyard while he described his plants and shrubs. He rarely gabs on the phone, though. In spite of its convenience, it's still just a novelty to Bill. To him, the phone is mostly a business tool that greatly increases sales and allows him to better serve his accounts.

Several people and companies attempted to give Bill a computer as a gift. One kind lady went so far as to set one up in Bill's house. Bill experimented with it, but all that he got out of it when he typed his name was "BBBBB" and "Poooorrtterr." That was the end of that. No way was he replacing his manual typewriter with a computer. He just laughed when I assured him that a computer would simplify his record keeping. "No it won't," he said, "because I won't have one of those contraptions in my home."

Bill may be a lot wiser than many of us when it comes to the use of high-tech gadgets. When I count the hours I've spent at the computer "saving time" only to have the program crash, I know in my heart that Bill may be the smart one to stick with pecking away at the keys on his manual typewriter. I've learned from Bill that a simple, gadget-free life can sometimes be a better one. He doesn't have to worry about answering e-mails or taping mindless television shows. He isn't constantly updating his computer and the software needed to run it. He is busy living life, meeting people one on one, face to face, and not carrying on conversations out in cyberspace. He takes the time to smell the roses or at least the dinner cooking. Why fix what isn't broken?

Every time someone in my family physically injures themselves, I tell a story Bill told me about the time he took a terrible spill on the sidewalk in front of a customer's house.

"I tripped and fell, landing on my chin," he states matter-of-factly. "Blood was everywhere. One of my customers drove me to the hospital and stayed by my side until the doctor could see me. I ended up with seven stitches. She wanted to drive me home afterwards so I could rest, but I wasn't finished with my selling day. I told her I'd rather be driven back to my territory."

And sure enough, Bill finished his eight-hour day, bandaged chin and all, staying a little longer than usual to make up for the time he spent at the hospital.

The story would have ended much differently if the same accident had happened to me. I would have gone home to bed, called my husband on the cordless, moaned that I was in too much pain to cook, and asked him to bring home a pizza. I've been known to do that after stubbing my toe or breaking a fingernail. Seven stitches could possibly buy me a week in bed. Then, I'd get out of bed only to use the restroom, get popcorn refills, and answer e-mails.

I've seen Bill confined to bed on only two occasions, and to see my unstoppable friend physically "broken" is heart wrenching. For the first fourteen years I knew him, Bill never took a day off from work. Nothing kept him home, not a cold, flu, arthritis, not even his intense migraine headaches. But after years of pounding the pavement with an excruciatingly painful back condition, Bill finally sought help from a doctor. After trying everything from oral medication to cortisone shots to physical therapy, his doctor said back surgery was the only way to stop the pain. He also let Bill know that there was the very real possibility he may not be able to walk again if the surgery wasn't successful. Unwilling to take such a risk, Bill put off the surgery. The days turned into weeks, weeks into months, months into years. Eventually the pain became so intense it outweighed the risks of surgery and Bill agreed to the operation.

The surgery was postponed until after the 1993 holiday

season because Bill wanted to conclude the year with top sales honors. Unfortunately, he had cancelled his health insurance a few years prior because he couldn't afford the premiums. To make matters worse, he had decided a few years back to take out a second mortgage on his paid-for house for some much-needed improvement projects. In 1990, he consolidated all his outstanding debt into one equity loan with a high interest loan company (i.e., loan shark) that solicited his business over the phone. The telemarketer convinced Bill it would make things easier to pool his financial obligations and only have one check to write. Unfortunately, the high interest on the new loan didn't leave him enough money to pay his property taxes, and so now he faced the real possibility of losing his home to the loan company or to the county for unpaid taxes.

Meanwhile, the back operation was scheduled for the end of January 1994. Bill's life was falling to pieces, physically and financially. One afternoon he swallowed his pride and told me of his dilemma. Here he was having back surgery, which might put an abrupt end to his only source of income — door-to-door sales. He didn't know if he would ever walk again, let alone make a living. To top it off, he didn't know if he would own a home to rehabilitate himself in.

My husband John and I had an immediate family meeting. We had recently refinanced our home to take advantage of lower interest rates, and, like Bill, we set aside extra money in the loan package for some home projects, including city-mandated sewer improvements. The day before my conversation with Bill, we had made an early payment of four thousand dollars to the city, leaving us with little cash with which to help Bill. What if we called the sewer office to get that check back and used the money instead as a down payment for the purchase of Bill's house? He could rent it from us for far less money than he was making in loan payments each month.

We approached Bill with our proposal. Before we could say more than a few words, he told us he had been thinking along the same lines. The next few days were a blur as we made phone calls, managed to get our check back, filled out dozens of documents, and finally secured the money to pay off Bill's high-interest loan, past-due property taxes, and other assorted debts. We then turned around and rented the house to Bill for much less than he had been paying for the loan.

It was frightening for us at the time to take on the financial risk of another mortgage because in 1994 we added child number four, Kevin Patrick, for a grand total of six mouths to feed. We were stretched to our financial limits. But as long as Bill made his portion, we could survive. If he was unable to work after his back surgery, I was prepared to work part-time at McDonald's, because in our hearts we felt good about what had transpired for two reasons: most importantly, it was a way to help our friend Bill, and, of course, it would be a good long-term investment for us.

Bill's surgery did go very well. The doctor ordered bed rest and restricted the use of stairs. Bill ignored the doctor's orders and rested only when pain forced him to. Remarkably, his strength returned rapidly, and after only two months Bill was anxious to reconnect with his Watkins accounts.

He began by selling over the telephone, and his loyal client base gladly placed their orders. (My fantasy of a two-month vacation from Watkins deliveries flew out the window.) Bill was happy to just be selling again but complained

that he dearly missed door-to-door sales. On the telephone, he found he "traveled" too quickly through his territory, missing out on the subtle delights involved in meeting one-on-one with his customers. No one believed it was possible, but in May 1994, only four months after his surgery, Bill was back at it, pounding the pavement. The doctors were truly amazed that anyone could be up and about so quickly, let alone someone with cerebral palsy.

Soon, his back surgery and time-off were a distant memory, and it was back to business for Bill and Shelly, and business was good.

The year 1997 brought new adventures for Bill and myself. The *Oregonian* article, just a little more than a year old, was still attracting new customers and media attention. ABC's *20/20* came out to film Bill's story, with plans to air it later in the year to more than twenty million viewers. Companies all over the country — even some from abroad — clamored for us to tell Bill's inspiring story at their conventions. Hollywood producers and actors expressed interest in making a movie of Bill's life. Book publishers called to see if I was interested in writing a book about him. Then, exactly one week after the *20/20* piece was filmed in late July, Bill stepped off the curb in front of his house and was sideswiped by a distracted driver. One split second changed Bill's life and mine forever.

Like victims of an earthquake remembering where they were when the big one hit, I remember Bill's accident and the events leading up to it as if they happened yesterday. The week started out insanely for me. I promised to help a friend with her daughter's wedding, a Japanese exchange student was arriving to stay with us, and we were busy packing for our annual family camping trip. On top of all this, I was watching two children for a friend, my house was a mess, and because of the trip I needed to deliver the Watkins products a couple of days early.

I headed to the grocery store with seven children. We did Bill's shopping and drove to his house to put away the groceries and clean. Michelle changed the sheets. Katrina scrubbed the bathroom. Tessa and Joey (a friend's son) dusted everything. Kevin and Kelsey (friend's daughter) played with the baby (Erica, our fifth). I supervised, hoping to get things cleaned as quickly as possible because Bill was due home around 2:30, when he would give me the exact directions for the deliveries.

Rarely did I ask Bill to modify delivery days; remember, he doesn't like change! Years of friendship softened him somewhat, and if a real need presented itself, Bill could be swayed a little. So knowing Bill usually typed the directions to the houses on Tuesdays, I asked him if he could dictate them to me when I came over to clean on Monday. (This would take about half an hour as opposed to the thirteen hours Bill normally spends typing directions.) He told me he had personal errands to run on Monday and would be home sometime after noon, at the latest 2:30. I told him I'd be at his house by 1:00, certain he'd be back no later than 1:30 as he always likes to be home when I am there.

One-thirty came and went. I was surprised, but figured he'd be home by 2:30 for sure. When 2:30 came and went, knowing how punctual he always is, I began to worry. Where could he be? By 3:00 we were finished cleaning and still no Bill. I began to panic. *Why hasn't he called? What on earth was the problem? A missed bus connection, a new customer? What? He's never late without calling.* I sent the children out to the back yard to play because they were getting restless, and I didn't want them to mess up the house.

A car pulled up and I ran to the door. It was my in-laws, Deborah and Gary Wood; Bill had hired them to do his yard work. They had come to drop off a receipt for a garden hose.

No, they hadn't seen Bill. They had worked in the yard that morning, but Bill had already left to run errands. While Gary, Deborah, and I stood on the porch talking about where Bill could be, a stranger approached the house. From here on out, everything seemed to happen in slow motion. The words that came out of the stranger's mouth sounded like a 45-rpm record played at 33 rpm. Everything was surreal, as if I was dreaming, except this dream was quickly turning into a nightmare.

"Bill was hit by a car this morning," the stranger said.

A stunned silence followed. Finally, I was able to activate my vocal chords.

"Is he okay? What happened? Do you know where he is? Who hit him? Is he badly injured?"

When I finally shut up long enough to hear an answer, the stranger said, "An ambulance took Bill away. His forehead was cut, and he was walking around and arguing with the ambulance driver about him not needing to go to the hospital. They finally convinced him to get into the ambulance." The stranger didn't know where they took Bill. I later found out that he was Bill's neighbor.

After thanking him, I went into the house, opened the phone book to the yellow pages, and proceeded to call hospital after hospital. Three phone calls in a row yielded no patient by the name of Bill Porter. At last, on my fourth attempt, Emanuel Hospital confirmed that a William Douglas Porter was admitted to the emergency room earlier in the day, and was transferred to the X-ray department. She wasn't sure where he was at the time. I ended the conversation and quickly loaded seven restless children into my van. Emanuel Hospital was only seven short minutes away.

Once there, I learned the gash on Bill's head required stitches, but his X ray indicated no other problems. However, because Bill appeared disoriented they felt it necessary to refer him to social services.

"Why didn't someone call me?" I wanted to know. Meanwhile, the children made the best of the situation by sliding down banisters and jumping on the sofas in the lobby; I attempted to contact social services and, of course, an answering machine was the only response I got. Upset because I didn't know what happened to Bill, I snapped at the children to "sit still." If he was discharged, then where is he? Why didn't he go home? I pleaded with the hospital receptionist to please try to reach the social service agent for me. Within minutes, the agent answered the page and I asked her what happened to Bill. She said she tried to convince him to go home and rest as he had taken quite a tumble. She offered to get him a cab. He'd refused, saying that it was only a few stitches and he had to finish some errands. *Oh no,* I thought, *there he goes again.* "If it isn't completely broken, why fix it?"

Since there was nothing else to accomplish at the hospital, I headed home with seven very hungry and cranky children. Naturally, I swung by Bill's in the hope that he would be there; no such luck. I tried to convince myself that he lost track of time after his accident, but realized that wasn't possible; this is Bill we're dealing with, after all. Surely he would remember his dear friend Shelly, and how worried sick she would be.

At 6:00 the phone rang. It was Bill.

"Where are you? Why haven't you called?" I asked.

His voice was slurred and it was extremely difficult to decipher his words. "I was hit by a car," he said.

"I know. I've been trying to find you. Where are you?" I demanded.

"I'm at Providence Hospital. I left my house this morning to run my errands downtown. I stepped onto the street and the next thing I knew there was a car coming at me and I went stumbling to the ground. The driver pulled out to make a left turn. He says he didn't see me because the sun was in his eyes. What kind of excuse is that?"

He sounded angry. I tried to calm him. "It was an accident, Bill. The driver must feel terrible. I wouldn't want to be in either one of your shoes. So, did he actually hit you?"

"I don't know. I think so. There were two people standing at the bus stop. One of them says he hit me. The other thinks he might have stopped just before hitting me and that it startled me and I fell. I'm pretty banged up for just a fall."

"I heard you got stitches. What else is wrong? Why are

you in the hospital? Why didn't you come home? Why didn't you call?"

"The ambulance insisted on taking me to the hospital. I thought it was a waste of time. They stitched up my head and sent me for X rays because my leg and back hurt. When they told me my X rays were clear, I figured it was time to go. Some social service agent wanted me to go home. I told her I was fine and I left."

"Why didn't you go home, Bill? Are you in pain?"

"Of course I'm in pain, but what else is new? Why should I go home for pain when there are things to be done?"

There was no use arguing. What I wanted to know was why Bill was calling from another hospital. He continued.

"I left the hospital and started my errands. I went to the allergy clinic and the bank. Each step got more and more painful. Soon I couldn't go on. I found myself collapsed on the sidewalk in excruciating pain. It felt like knives were stabbing my hips. A passerby called an ambulance. I didn't argue this time. They brought me to Providence Hospital, and they are taking me in for more X rays soon."

I told Bill I was so grateful he called and that he was okay for the most part. He cut off my ramblings to tell me the real reason he called was to give me the delivery directions! Lo and behold, he proceeded with house number one: "Go out Dosch Park Road; take a right on Bridlemile Lane. . . ." What was I to do but write them down? He continued until I heard the nurse in the background saying, "Mr. Porter, we really need to wheel you to X-ray now." I smiled to myself as he said good-bye, promising to call me back with the rest of the directions as soon as he was back in his room.

The next phone call from Bill informed me of his X-ray results: he had fractured his hip in the accident. The break was in such an awkward spot that it didn't surprise the X-ray technician that the other hospital had missed it. The doctor would be performing surgery shortly, so Bill had to quickly recite the rest of the delivery directions. The pain medications slurred his voice to the point where I could barely understand him. Fortunately, I had been delivering for him long enough that I was familiar with the area and the clients. I assured Bill I would not get lost and that all of his Watkins products would be delivered properly and promptly.

The next two months would prove to be the most challenging in Bill's life since the death of his mother. He arrived home from the hospital one week later, battered and bruised but in good spirits. Once again he was given strict orders to use his walker and stay off of the stairs. Social services brought him a portable commode to discourage him from using the upstairs bathroom.

This time he didn't heal as quickly as he did after back surgery. Two days after arriving home, he suffered a terrible setback. Bill called me saying he felt dizzy and 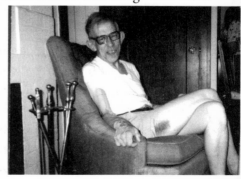 nauseous. I had been at his house only two hours earlier to take pictures of his injuries — a black eye and badly bruised legs — and joking about making a poster that read, "You should see what I did to the other guy!"

I sped back to Bill's and helped him get to bed. We both figured he needed rest. Shortly after I returned home, Bill's neighbor called.

"Bill is in trouble," he said. "Can you please come back? I can't find my key to his house."

By the time I got there, Bill was vomiting and his chest was tight. He was dizzy and pale. It really scared me to see him looking that way. I called 911 and an ambulance took him back to the hospital. I locked up his house, went home, and waited to hear from the doctors.

The next six weeks were a blur. Bill's equilibrium was so poor he wasn't able to walk down the hospital corridor. The hospital staff felt he shouldn't go home anytime soon; they wanted him to spend time at an adult care facility where he could have twenty-four-hour attention and intense physical therapy. Bill was adamantly opposed to the idea. He wanted to know, "Why can't someone stay with me at my house? Why can't a nurse visit me for therapy twice a week like the hospital said originally?"

I explained that we were all worried about his dizziness, about the risk of falling down if he were home alone, and about the danger of re-injuring his hip. At a care facility, he would receive physical therapy twice a day verses two times a week at home. He'd get well that much faster. I wished I could help him around the clock, but I was scheduled to be out of town and I had my children to look after. I was glad to come over often, but he needed much more than I could give him.

"Please," I begged him. "I would worry much less about you if you stayed in the hands of professionals." Furthermore, Medicare paid almost all the cost of an adult-care facility stay, but would cover very little or none of the cost of at-home care.

After much pleading, Bill reluctantly agreed to stay at the facility. The move almost broke his spirit; he retreated inside himself, as if the world had given up hope on him. No amount of humor seemed to change his attitude. From Bill's point of view, it must have appeared that the establishment finally had him where they wanted him his entire life — in an institution. From our perspective, nothing could be farther from the truth; we wanted him out of the facility as soon as possible. We wanted him well and out here with us, inspiring us as he always has.

I can't remember when things turned around. After many weeks, Bill slowly climbed out of his shell. He stopped complaining "I don't belong here" and "I know I'll never see my front porch again" and started concentrating on regaining his strength. Exactly one day before his sixty-fifth birthday, he received the best present ever: a ride home! His condition was greatly improved and it looked like things might get back to normal.

One month later, Bill felt he was ready to reclaim his territory in person. I remember the wet day in October when I worried about every step, every curb, and every passing car. That evening I called Bill to ask how it went. He sounded very different; there was no spunk or verve in his voice. Words were uttered from Bill's lips that I never thought I'd hear. "I can't do it, Shelly. I tried, but I just can't."

Bill told me what happened that day: "I took the bus to my territory and started walking. Each step became more and more painful until I finally had to sit down on the curb and rest. Before the day was half through, I realized my door-to-door days were over. It took every ounce of strength I had just to make it back to the bus stop. I can't walk my route anymore. I don't know what I'm going to do."

I couldn't sleep that night thinking about what appeared to be my friend's broken spirit. How would this problem be resolved, I wondered? I didn't have to wonder too long, though, because the next morning Bill called with an idea:

"I've made up my mind, Shelly. I'll sell over the phone. I did it three years ago when my back went out and I can do it again."

And Bill Porter did just that! I can attest to the fact that he was every bit as successful, if not more, selling over the phone as he was selling door-to-door. I made his deliveries and he sold so many Watkins products that I had to enlist John and our children to help with deliveries.

By the time ABC's *20/20* segment on Bill aired on December 12, 1997, just five months after his accident, Bill was back to his old self. Most of his successful routines were reinstituted. If something worked in the past, Bill didn't see any need to change it. If change was forced upon him, like a broken hip or back, he learned to adapt his behavior, but only slightly.

Stubborn determination keeps Bill focused and on track. I remember him lamenting that his favorite team was playing on a Saturday afternoon and how he would have to miss the game because it was during "callbacks." I reminded him he was his own boss, and he could rearrange his hours, watch the game, and do "callbacks" later. He looked at me like I was crazy. I  should have known better than to try to help Bill Porter fix something that wasn't broken.

There Are No Obstacles

The first speaking engagement Bill and I contracted for was titled *Overcoming Obstacles: The Bill Porter Story.* I wanted to prepare fully for the occasion, so with notebook in hand, I asked Bill a few questions. "Bill, I want you to tell me all your obstacles."

After a long silence, I looked up from my notebook to see Bill staring at me. I repeated the question.

"Shelly," Bill stated emphatically, "how many times do I have to tell you and everyone else? I don't have any obstacles. Ask me another question."

We played this cat-and-mouse game for fifteen minutes, with me cleverly rephrasing the question to trick the answer I wanted out of Bill: cerebral palsy, a lack of muscle coordination, an aching back, a speech impediment. I wasn't having any luck; Bill wouldn't play the game with me. He sincerely believes he doesn't have any obstacles of any kind.

I knew audiences admired Bill because he overcame major obstacles in his life, and I wanted to satisfy them. They thought of him as a hero, an inspiration, a man who overcame tremendous odds. After learning from Bill's example, my hope was that audience members with obstacles would be encouraged to overcome them.

However, Bill's stubbornness forced me to change my approach to the speech. Instead of talking about how Bill overcame his obstacles, I was forced to speak about Bill's "perceived" lack of obstacles. The word "obstacle" simply doesn't exist in Bill's vocabulary. He understands an obstacle to be something that totally blocks one from reaching a destination or goal, but the fact of the matter is, Bill never encounters "obstacles" because he always reaches his goal, whether it be a physical location or a sales quota. He is simply unstoppable.

When I was a child, my parents said I could be anything I wanted, the President of the United States or an Olympic swimmer. While I believed they were sincere, I never really took them too seriously; I felt the odds were extremely slim that either could actually happen. I appreciated their confidence in me, but I set my sights on what I considered more realistic, attainable goals such as a college education, a large, loving family, and a rewarding career. (In light of recent presidencies and elections, who really wants to be President of the United States, anyway?)

On the other hand, the opposite is true with Bill. He can quote verbatim what his mother said to him when he was eight years old: "Bill, you can accomplish anything you want, if you just set your mind to it." Bill believed his mother whole-heartedly. I see this positive attitude in Bill's approach to every stumbling block (not obstacle, mind you) he encounters. The following story is a typical example.

A few years ago, an especially cold and icy storm dropped out of Alaska onto the streets of Portland. Bill heard about the storm from the television weather forecasters. Being the complete optimist, however, he figured the forecasters were over estimating its strength. Bill puts a positive spin on weather forecasts in the summertime as well. When the forecasters predict highs in the nineties, he tells me, "I think cool." The weather is very important to Bill because it determines what he wears and whether he should carry an overcoat or an umbrella. On this particular stormy day, Bill dressed appropriately and made his scheduled rounds. Every customer he encountered told him he should call it a day and head for home before the freezing rain started. Bill thought it was a perfect day for door-to-door sales because, as he says, "When the weather gets really nasty, more customers are home."

Finally, after he exceeded his daily quota, he was ready to head home. Unfortunately, Bill didn't outguess the weatherman this time; the buses had stopped running due to the storm and Bill had to hitchhike home. Not only was it bitterly cold and wet, the roads were dangerously slick. By the time he reached the steep driveway leading to his front door, it had frozen into a sheet of black ice as slippery as an ice skating rink. Bill tried again and again to get up his driveway, but he kept falling down. His shoes couldn't get any traction. After several painful falls, he got down on all fours, crawled to his front door, turned the key, stepped inside, and at last proceeded to prepare his dinner while he watched the weather forecast for the next day.

The image of Bill crawling up his driveway on all fours is forever etched in my mind. When I scolded him for not calling for help, he said, "What's the big deal? Nobody could have made it up that driveway without getting down on all fours."

Another example of Bill's refusal to submit to obstacles takes place every evening after he finishes dinner. As I mentioned in an earlier chapter, Bill is wise enough to hire employees when the job at hand is too time-consuming or too difficult for his physical abilities. For instance, I deliver customer's orders for him in my car because he doesn't drive; a gardener keeps his yard neat because it takes him too much time and effort; a housekeeper keeps Bill's home neat and well-stocked with his favorite foods (mostly frozen). I have been Bill's housekeeper for fifteen years and now my children help perform the task.

However, even though Bill is familiar with the benefits of employing assistants, I can't convince him to hire a secretary to type his orders. It just pains me to watch him peck away with one finger. Even a mediocre typist could prepare his orders in a matter of minutes. Bill spends hours pecking away, insists on doing all his own typing, and often types superflu-

ous special delivery instructions with each order. *Go down driveway. Open the gate. Leave the package by the back door. Close the gate behind you.* I don't need such detailed instructions and told him so, but he continues to add them anyway.

After the *Oregonian* article appeared, which included a vivid description of Bill's poor typing skills, multiple offers came in for free typing services from professional typists. Bill wouldn't accept any of them; he has to type all orders to ensure accuracy. And actually, Bill seems to enjoy himself as he finger-types each order. This is just another example of Bill turning an obstacle as painstaking and tedious as typing into a form of relaxation where he can reflect on his day and plan out the next.

The following incident temporarily had me believing that Bill's optimistic approach to obstacles was coming to an end. Bill and I credit Tom Hallman's article in the *Oregonian,* "Life of a Salesman," with creating major positive changes in his life. However, very few people know that when the article first appeared on Sunday, November 27, 1995, Bill was extremely upset by it. Personally, I was ecstatic that so many people were learning about my noble and brave friend Bill Porter. Sure, I was a little worried that the detailed description of Bill's handicaps might initially hurt Bill's feelings, but not to the extreme that it did.

When I called him the morning the article came out, he was fit to be tied. He believed he hadn't been treated fairly. He felt the article portrayed him as a freak. The reporter's use of the word "twisted" to describe his body was what irked Bill the most. Keep in mind that Bill Porter is, for good reason, a very proud man. He is a dignified and gracious human being who doesn't see himself as suffering from the physical symptoms associated with cerebral palsy.

I spent the next hour-and-a-half explaining to Bill that Tom Hallman's article was very well written.

"Tom picked the word 'twisted,'" I gently said, "because he needed to paint a picture with words and to aid readers of the article in understanding what cerebral palsy is and the physical limitations that often accompany the disease."

Bill retorted, "My friends and customers don't see me that way. They don't think my body is twisted. Why did he have to pick that word?"

I had never seen Bill so upset in all the years I'd known him. My belief in Bill's ability to overcome all obstacles appeared to fly out the window. I couldn't calm him down. Furthermore, he was annoyed by the vivid description of his nightstand. Mr. Hallman described it as "littered with medications for a body that was in constant pain."

"I am not in constant pain," Bill exclaimed.

"But you are in constant pain," I said. "Step away from yourself for a minute. You have migraines at least two days a week. Your arthritis flares up and your back aches on almost a daily basis. The rest of the world, including doctors, calls that constant pain."

After a few days went by, Bill was still hurt and bitter about the *Oregonian* article. Tom Hallman was very concerned about Bill's response; he expected the exact opposite reaction. He truly has the greatest respect and admiration for Bill, and he asked me if I could speak to Bill and straighten out the misunderstanding. He wanted Bill to realize that his intentions were honorable. He simply wanted the readers of the article to comprehend the full extent of Bill's physical condition so they could more fully appreciate Bill's greatness. The situation was a catch-22: Bill doesn't think he has physical limitations or obstacles, and, being an excellent journalist, Mr. Hallman was obligated to portray the facts accurately, and the fact of the matter is...Bill Porter has cerebral palsy.

It wasn't until Bill learned that more than seven hundred readers wrote, e-mailed, or phoned the *Oregonian* wanting to become his customers that Bill finally began to see things differently. "Tom really didn't mean any harm," he stated later. Bill was pleasantly overwhelmed with the arduous task of typing up all those new orders with one finger. He soon broke all existing sales records for Watkins products in the Pacific Northwest. "I guess my back does hurt once in a while," he later admitted.

Most recently, serious health problems have forced Bill to curtail travel by airplane. It wasn't easy for him to admit that there was an obstacle that could best him. Fortunately, my husband and I found innovative, high-tech solutions to the problem.

The discovery that flying wasn't healthy for Bill couldn't have come at a worse time in our busy speaking schedule. We were booked solid for engagements at Amway, Watkins, Disney, Nike, and other companies. We were definitely on a roll. Bill enjoyed the luxurious accommodations, and I thrived on the opportunity to travel and speak.

Then it happened — Bill couldn't catch his breath during a flight to Atlanta as I slept soundly next to him. Bill thought that death wasn't far away. Of course, he didn't bother to nudge me and let me assist him. He made it through his state of panic with the aid of an inhaler, but the incident was incredibly frightening for Bill.

This shortness of breath wasn't new to him; he often experienced it after walking a few blocks. But after resting momentarily and using an inhaler, he was always able to catch his breath and continue. Bill called them "breathing episodes" (in other words, "no big deal"). The doctors believed the shortness of breath was due to progressive, fibrotic lung disease. This ailment originated from an acid-reflux condition, whereby stomach acids cause scarring of the lung tissue. In layman's terms, Bill's lungs weren't capable of processing the oxygen his body needed. The poor air quality on long airplane flights exacerbated the situation.

To compound the problem, Bill began to experience "panic attacks." They occurred whenever he felt he was in a situation where he might lose his breath. These attacks caused Bill's lungs to hyperventilate, thereby triggering a "breathing episode." Bill went through a tug-of-war over whether to continue traveling or give in to his illness and stay near the safety of home. Despite being the brave man who he is, he took one more flight to the East Coast and then called it quits; no more air travel.

Personally, I was devastated by Bill's refusal to travel by plane. I pictured my speaking career coming to an abrupt halt. I thought, *Who wants Shelly without Bill?* Prior to putting the suitcase in the attic, I did some brainstorming with my computer-literate husband. John saw no reason why we couldn't use the latest advances in digital photography and the Internet to "virtually" present Bill on stage with me. Now, when Bill can't be present, I keep a live telephone connection with him while I'm on stage. This way Bill and I can banter back and forth. Bill went along with the program because he knew how much I love public speaking and he loves the publicity, which translates into increased sales.

The presentations, with live audio and/or video feeds to Bill, have gone extremely well. The audience's response to Bill's "virtual" presence has been equal to the responses we received when he was on stage with me.

At the end of most presentations, I ask the audience what they feel is the greatest obstacle Bill overcame. The responses run the gamut: cerebral palsy, back surgery, declining health, death of his mother, inability to drive. The list goes on. I sometimes write these obstacles on a large chalkboard as they are spoken. Then turning to Bill on live video or by telephone, I go down the list: "Was cerebral palsy an obstacle? Was your mother's death an obstacle?" With unwavering conviction, he dismisses each so-called "obstacle" one by one. "I don't believe I have any obstacles at all," he says time and again.

The number of people inspired by Bill Porter's life story astounds me. Incredibly, many of these people only know of him from the twenty-minute segment on *20/20* or the *Oregonian* newspaper article. Since I've been an employee and friend of Bill's for many years, it's only natural that he has inspired me. Nearly every day I have watched him routinely conquer greater obstacles than I have faced in my entire life.

Nonetheless, I have struggled with personal obstacles that, at times, have made me feel inadequate and frustrated with myself. Experiences in my youth, for example, affected my attitude towards money and material wealth. When I was twelve years old, my family moved from Portland to Kauai, a small island in Hawaii. My parents moved there for employment that never materialized, and consequently we learned to make do with what little money we had. Out of necessity, my mother learned to bake bread from scratch and grow much of our food in a garden. We hung our laundry in the sun to save electricity. Graciously, we accepted gifts of tropical fruit from friends and neighbors who knew the gifts were much appreciated.

Attire on the islands is much more casual than on the mainland, but we dressed casually because we had no choice. The money simply wasn't available to replace our plastic flip-flops when they became thin and chewed up. In spite of this, I joked about running around in my bare feet like a native child, all the time aware of the endless array of spiffy shoes lining the department store shelves in Honolulu and on the mainland. After all, I was a teenage *houle* (Hawaiian for Caucasian) from the mainland who, at times, longed for a more comfortable lifestyle. Although I cherish my years living on Kauai, I know that's where I adopted a reluctance to spend money that has caused some strife in my marriage over the years.

After the birth of our first child, John and I decided it was time for me to quit my job so I could be a full-time homemaker. It meant changing our lifestyle as we made the shift from two incomes to one. It was a frightening time, but it felt right for us. We scrimped and saved to make house payments on our first home and pay back our school loans. We tightened our belts and took a gigantic leap of faith.

Like my mother on Kauai, I went into survival mode, but instead of raising a garden and baking my own bread, I became an expert at clipping coupons and finding sales. A friend introduced me to thrift stores and garage sales. Before I knew it, my calendar was full: Friday mornings — garage sales, before anyone got there; Saturday afternoons — garage sales, when people wanted to get rid of their stuff at half price; Tuesday — thrift stores, when the "new" used merchandise was put out; Wednesday night — groceries, when the meat and dairy section were marked half-price just prior to the expiration date.

Wherever there was a bargain, I could sniff it out. Intuitively, I knew when to step on the brakes and turn for a sale. I developed a reputation as the "thrift queen," and I was proud of it. I felt that I enabled us to live beyond our means because of my keen eye for bargains. When someone complimented me one time on a new outfit, I proudly responded, "I got this suit at the Value Village for just $1.98, and the shoes were only 99 cents." When company came over, it was always an opportunity for me to "show and tell" my latest findings, from furnishings to closets full of clearance items. I was well prepared for upcoming birthday parties, showers, or weddings.

My husband appreciated the fact that I didn't have to shop at the finest stores, but he pointed out that it wasn't wise to buy something we didn't need just because it was a bargain. "Do you really need ten photo albums for weddings we haven't even been invited to yet?" he asked.

It became increasingly embarrassing for him when we went out to dinner with friends from work and I pulled out a stack of coupons when the waiter brought the check, or the time our four-year-old daughter blurted out to a lady at church that "Mommy bought this dress for me at the Goodwill."

After John's income rose and I started bringing in extra money by working part-time for Bill, John felt it was time to buy new living room furniture. I disagreed. "Sure, our used furniture doesn't match and has a few stains from children and pets, but the same thing would happen to new furniture, so why waste the money? Besides, there's an estate sale coming up next weekend and we might find something there."

John nevertheless insisted that I budget for a new sofa and although I promised I would, I secretly continued to spend any extra money on "necessary" sale items.

My passion for bargain hunting turned into an obsession. I was addicted like a compulsive gambler, always thinking the next great treasure was just around the corner. I had passed up Saturday outings with the family because that was when the best garage sales occurred. John grew more and more frustrated with my addiction. He felt it was taking precious time away from the family and, anyway, was getting downright embarrassing.

The situation came to a head one night when we made a date; just the two of us would go out on a Saturday night and spend some much needed time without the little ones. I decided to leave the planning to John because if I made the plans, a coupon for dinner or dessert would surely be involved.

John suggested we go to a movie that we both anxiously wanted to see. He said, "I'll call the babysitter so we can catch the seven o'clock show." My mind began to whirl and calculate: *The 7:00 P.M. show? What is he thinking? This is crazy. I can't go to a full-priced show.*

"John, honey," I said, "can't we go to the matinee instead? It's so much cheaper."

That was the straw that broke the camel's back. He looked me in the eye and said, "I can't believe you, Shelly. You've got five hundred dollars worth of candy hidden in a bureau drawer. You spend over two thousand dollars a year on gifts. But you won't pay three dollars extra to see a movie on a Saturday night. You complain about me never planning a date and when I do, you complain about that. We can afford the three dollars, I assure you."

The candy drawer and gift budget were an exaggeration, I rationalized to myself, and technically three dollars times two meant we would spend more like six dollars or even ten dollars more than a discounted matinee, especially if you counted the popcorn. I could see that I was carrying my thriftiness too far, but I couldn't stop myself. It was becoming a real obstacle in our marriage and family. I knew I had to change, but no amount of logic dispensed by my husband could stop me. I turned to my old friend Bill for help and inspiration. He has less expendable money than John and I, but he doesn't feel the need to shop "cheap." He lives from month to month and is content and comfortable with his simpler life.

A story Bill told me helped cure my compulsion to shop for bargains. While preparing a speech, I asked him what he remembered about his early childhood in San Francisco. I expected him to talk about persecution from other children or the physical pain associated with cerebral palsy. Wrong again, Shelly! Bill couldn't (or perhaps refused to) recall *any* painful memories. It was a happy, trouble-free time for him.

"I remember the teachers would take us out for sunbaths on the deck for a half-hour each day. The sun felt great on my skin. The teachers would tell us to roll over after fifteen minutes were up. I remember one evening my mom told me it was time to take a bath. I told her I didn't need to because I had already taken a bath, a sunbath. She laughed, but made me take a real bath with soap and water!"

I looked at Bill while he talked and I could see in his eyes how he truly cherished his joyous child-hood. It brought tears of joy to my eyes. He is blessed with the ability to dwell on the positive and thinks of obstacles as exciting challenges.

I drifted off to my own childhood while he continued talking. I imagined myself on the beaches of Kauai with the surf up to my knees, waving back to my family on the beach. It was a beauti-ful, oft-repeated scene in my childhood. The sun and water felt so good. I knew without a doubt that my parents loved me and I loved them. It suddenly struck me how lucky I was to have grown up in a family that loved each other, no matter how much money was or was not in the bank. I also realized that, like Bill, I had no real obstacles; I wasn't handicapped because my family didn't have a lot of money. Rather, I was blessed because they loved me, just as my present family loves me and I love them. I finally saw clearly that I had allowed money — or the lack of it — to become an obstacle, an obsession, instead of a challenge. I didn't have to go overboard to save money and hoard bargain items. I had something you can't buy with money — love.

It has taken years, but with Bill as an example, I have changed my attitude towards money. Today, the last thing on my list of things I want to do is shop! (Besides, we could probably live for years off of the stuff I have in storage.) Now and then, I take a deep breath and treat the entire family to a full priced movie. Saturdays are now reserved for creating happy family memories. On hot summer days, we've been known to go to the beach, play in the surf, and sunbathe. From Bill, I learned that I really don't have obstacles left over from my childhood, only challenges that require perseverance and time to overcome. Thank you, Bill Porter.

Live Your Values

B ill is often asked, "What makes you tick? What makes you get up day after day, don a business suit, and sell door-to-door when you could stay home and collect disability payments?"

He answers, "I knew there was something I could do. I felt it deep inside. My mother told me I could do anything I set out to do and I believed her. I set out to work and nothing could make me take my eyes off that goal. When I was let go from the jobs the unemployment office set me up with, I was frustrated and discouraged, but I wouldn't let those feelings fester. I pushed them aside and kept going back. Eventually, I knew the right job would come my way. You must have faith in yourself and work hard. I learned that from my mother, my father, and God."

I marvel at the inner strength Bill Porter mustered during

the 1980s when he cared for his ill mother and continued to work each day. "I had to go to work. I had to pay the bills," he'll tell you. Bill's admirable character traits are built upon a deep, internal value system.

Shortly before his mother passed away, I was asked to volunteer time for a youth group at my church. The goal of the group was to introduce young women to values they could use today and carry with them their entire life. Those values were: faith, divine nature, individual worth, knowledge, choice and accountability, good works, and integrity.

We had the girls choose someone they knew personally who exemplified the seven values and discuss how they were manifested. Well-respected parents, teachers, grandparents, and friends were commonly cited as examples. To the surprise of the girls, I chose Bill Porter because more than anyone I know, he dramatically demonstrates the belief and practice of these seven values. In fact, he has believed and practiced them since childhood, when his parents taught him the importance of possessing the kind of internal values that one can rely on every day all through life. Bill's value system allowed him to function successfully in the face of major obstacles.

When it was my turn to discuss why I chose Bill as my example, I went down the list of values and talked about Bill's relationship with each one.

✎ Faith

Irene Porter was a deeply religious woman. She taught her son to love God's wisdom in very practical terms, not abstractly, but by action, by the way one deals with all aspects of life, positive or negative. Irene didn't take the good things in life for granted; she gave thanks for every good turn of events, and she didn't see misfortunes as unlucky, insurmountable coincidences. Pouting or bemoaning one's downcast state were not options.

The Porter family attended church every Sunday where they prayed and gave thanks to a loving Heavenly Father who blessed their lives. Irene had faith that God didn't make mistakes; Bill's cerebral palsy was a part of Bill and thus a gift from the heavens above. In her heart, she believed God loved the Porter family and watched over them at every juncture. Irene taught Bill that faith carries one through the toughest of times. Bill learned that faith in God is synonymous with faith in humankind, which allowed him to see his customers as brothers and sisters.

Divine Nature

Irene and Ernest never doubted that Bill was a child of God who inherited divine qualities and gifts. He was taught that he had an obligation to discover and share these gifts. Irene taught him to be patient; it takes time to discover all God has given us. After many years of searching, Bill found he had a gift for selling, for gaining the trust of others because he earned it. Along his route, his friends and customers received more than products

and smiles; they received from Bill an ability to recognize their own divine gifts and qualities.

🖎 *Individual Worth*

Irene felt it was a shame that parents of disabled children didn't recognize that a handicap can be a blessing in disguise. She understood the feelings of despair and sorrow, as she was initially devastated to learn her baby had cerebral palsy. But she quickly realized that Bill was special, that he was born into this world to teach important lessons to others. She believed her son was infinitely worthy of living in society, not in a hospital where his purpose on earth would be squelched. Consequently, Bill never developed an inferiority complex or a feeling of being handicapped. His mission was to be the best he could be, thereby inspiring others to learn by example that anything is possible.

🖎 *Knowledge*

Bill learned from his parents that knowledge is the key to a successful life. When Bill was diagnosed with cerebral palsy, Ernest and Irene educated themselves about the disease. Ernest quit his job as a salesman and found employment with a school for handicapped children, while Irene spent countless hours volunteering for United Cerebral Palsy. The Porters fought the establishment for years to get Bill into public schools. They knew that Bill needed a good education if he was ever going to make it on his own.

When Bill finally found work with Watkins, Incorporated,

he learned everything he could about the company and their products. From his parents, Bill knew that one must thoroughly acquaint oneself about a subject before taking an action, such as selling door-to-door. Once a door is opened, Bill feels it's his duty to answer any questions about any products in his catalog. He educated himself about the industry as a whole and consistently bests the competition. He perfected the art of selling his products with a "money-back guarantee," which enlarged his client list and eventually made him the top sales producer in the Pacific Northwest.

He memorized the shopping habits and the likes and dislikes of more than five hundred clients. He is able to recite the names of clients who use vanilla when they bake and which ones insist on biodegradable soaps. Knowledge is power to Bill, and he never stops learning.

☙ Choice and Accountability

Bill Porter certainly didn't choose to be born with cerebral palsy, but he and his parents had a choice of how to respond to the hand they'd been dealt. Many doctors and well-meaning friends suggested institutionalizing Bill. They told the Porters that there were many risks in keeping Bill at home. Instead, Irene and Ernest chose to love, nurture, and raise their child at home in spite of guaranteed hardships and sacrifices. They knew their medical bills would skyrocket and society wouldn't look kindly upon a family with a disabled child at home. Such children were to be hidden away in sanitariums and hospitals. But the choice to keep Bill was made without hesitation or regret.

Bill learned early on that choices exist; choices give one character and personality and distinguish good from evil. The knowledge that he had options was especially valuable to Bill when he first searched for employment.

"You have a choice, Bill," Irene told him. "You can get up and march right back down to that unemployment office and show them you're determined or stay home and stew." In theory it sounds simple, but many of us don't exercise our right to choose. Yet not making the right choice can lead to dead-end jobs and unfulfilled lives.

The knowledge that he had the power to pick and choose empowered Bill. When he deliberately chooses to ring a doorbell, he is formidable. One customer relates that when she saw Bill approach her house, she actually hid on the back porch and didn't answer the door. Bill knew she was at home and proceeded to knock on her back door. "I know you're home," he shouted. Out of complete embarrassment, the lady came out of hiding and bought a slew of products. Her husband read her the riot act when he came home.

"Why on God's earth did you buy from him when I told you not to?" he complained.

In her defense, she replied, "He's so upbeat and determined it's impossible to say no to him."

When the husband called to cancel the order, Bill guaranteed his money back in full if he wasn't satisfied. They are now long-time customers who welcome him into their home with open arms — and checkbooks.

🕮 Good Works

"Let your light so shine before men, that they may see your good works, and glorify your Father which is in heaven" (Matthew 5:16). Bill truly is a shining light in a dark world. He has spent his whole life working hard, struggling to learn everything he needed to become and stay independent. He is very much aware of and thankful for all the people who have come into his life to help him out. True, many of them receive a paycheck from Bill (remember, he is fiercely independent). He has accepted a few kind acts without payment: dinners from the ladies at church after his car accident, discounts on home improvements, new carpeting, and a sprinkler system, to mention a few.

Over the years, I have seen Bill watch for opportunities to "pay it forward." When a young teen who worked at a Wendy's Bill frequented was hit by a car, Bill was so concerned about her recovery he sent her flowers and chocolates and made numerous phone calls. On our business trips around the country, Bill always remembered to bring home thoughtful gifts for friends. He bought sweet smelling soaps and lotions for his physical therapist and souvenirs for his neighbors. I've seen him purchase candy from the kids selling door-to-door and then turn right around and give it back to them for resale or to eat themselves. Bill just shrugs his shoulders and says that chocolate gives him migraines anyway.

🕮 Integrity

When Bill sells a product to a client, there is never a hint of deception; he simply isn't capable of taking advantage of another human being. If you order a product from Bill, then you receive exactly what he promised, guaranteed by Bill and Watkins. To some business people, this righteous attitude may seem naive or unrealistic but it works; just look at his sales figures. When Bill reviews invoices in the evening, he sincerely looks out for his customers' interest. (Don't get me wrong; Bill loves the bottom line, too.) Every invoice is scanned to ensure that the numbers match up with the products.

In addition to delivering products for Bill, I was assigned the task of refunding overpayments of even a few cents. In Bill's mind, two cents is no different from two hundred dollars; it's a matter of principle. Integrity takes precedence over money at all times. Integrity is the sphere that all of his business transactions revolve around. According to Bill, messing with honesty and integrity would cause widespread doom and gloom.

✎ Brady Family Values

Bill's values are directly attributable to Irene's patient teachings, and I could just as well have chosen her as my example of a person who exemplifies the seven values we wished to impart upon the young girls at our church. She reminds me of how profoundly important it is for parents to teach their children well and to give them a value system they can believe in and carry with them through good times — and bad. My husband and I try to teach these same values to our children. One evening many years ago, my family sat down

at the kitchen table and discussed at length what our family mission should be. Knowing we couldn't include all the goals our large family hoped to accomplish, thoughts were openly shared and discussed and accepted or rejected. We narrowed the list to read:

Brady Family Mission

1. Be together forever.
2. Daddy and Mommy will watch over the children.
3. We will always be able to depend on each other in times of need.
4. We will always take the time to listen to each other.

We wrote the mission statement on a large piece of construction paper and hung it on our refrigerator. Ten years and four children later, this worn poster remains there today. Over the years as new goals were set — *Be kind, serve others, be thankful, love our neighbors, be honest* — we printed them on paper and taped them to the walls of the kitchen.

Although Bill and I belong to different faiths, we both believe in a higher power, one that includes us all as members of a large extended family, a family that loves and teaches each other. A verse I recently read encapsulates Bill Porter's life for me:

"...and let us run with patience the race that is set before us, looking unto Jesus the author and finisher of our faith" (Hebrews 12:1,2).

That is how I see Bill Porter — patiently running a race, a race he is winning because of values his parents and God taught him. May the race continue to be long and fruitful for Bill, for I believe he is a true hero in the eyes of humanity and God.

LETTERS
Things You've Given Bill Porter

T hrough more than four decades, Bill trudged the streets and
hills of Portland, Oregon, slightly bent, right arm pulled
close in, left hand clutching his briefcase, walking, knocking on
doors. He was an anonymous figure, known only to those on his
sales route and perhaps to curious visitors to the neighborhood.

An article written by Tom Hallman, Jr., for the Portland
Oregonian on November 27, 1995, introduced Bill Porter to a
wider world and inspired articles in *Reader's Digest* and *Positive
Living Magazine*. Television came next, with features on Bill
appearing on *CBS This Morning* and eventually ABC's *20/20*.
Millions of viewers watched and wept, and Bill's segment got the
largest viewer response in the history of *20/20*.

The response has touched Bill deeply. As the letters poured
in, he began to see a glimpse of an additional purpose to his life.
Bill and I would sit together in his living room reading every
single letter. Tears came to our eyes as we read the heart-felt out-
pourings of pain and joy from our new friends. Bill commented
how these letters gave him so much hope and strength. It was
like a circle of love and inspiration, confirming that what you
give away comes back tenfold.

Choosing which letters to include here was one of the most
difficult tasks we faced in putting this book together. Thank
you to all who wrote, and know that each and every letter is precious to Bill and to me.

December 1, 1998

Dear Mr. Porter,

I believe this is the first time in my 44 years that I have been moved to respond to a TV show. After seeing your story on 20/20 last week, I simply had to write to let you know how inspirational you are. I don't think anyone could have watched and learned about you without feeling moved. You are an uncommon and exceptional human being, though I'm certain that your modesty prevents you from even acknowledging that you are special in any way. This is just another facet of you that makes you so remarkable.

How lucky you were to have a mother who could instill such quiet confidence in you, and how lucky she, to have such a caring and hardworking son to look after her in her later years. You can be sure that before her cruel disease robbed her of her personality, she was indeed proud of you and grateful for all of your efforts on her behalf. Who wouldn't be proud to have such a son. You both completed each other's lives.

This world is in desperate need of positive role models and heroes, and while I'm sure you are uncomfortable with this praise and feel it is unwarranted, you are indeed someone that all of us can look up to. Your work ethic and determined spirit is the "right stuff" of which we see so little these days.

Thank you for renewing my faith in mankind you are wonderful!

I wish you good health, continued success in your business endeavors and most of all, happiness you have earned it and certainly deserve it!

Abby
Scarborough, Ontario

Mr. Porter,

I would just like to say that in a world where so many look for the smallest reasons to give up you are an inspiration. Not for what you have overcome but for showing the rare traits of determination and personal pride. I admire you, not for the adversities you have overcome but for your GOOD SOUL. The world needs more people like you.

Thomas W. Newton
New Carlisle, Ohio

April 12, 1998

Dear Mr. Porter,

My name is Pam Noblet, and I'm 17 years old. A couple of months ago I saw a 20/20 special about you. Right away I felt proud to know that TV has something positive on it. I wanted to find out how to write to you, so I wrote on the computer to 20/20. They replied and gave me your address. The reason why I'm writing is to tell you that you remind me a lot of my friend Matt.

Matt also has Cerebral Palsy, but he's in a wheelchair. Matt has enough strength to lead an entire football team. I met Matt about three years ago through a mutual friend. To tell you the truth, the first thing I noticed about Matt is not the wheelchair but his great big smile. Over the years that I've known him I've become really fond and protective of him. Matt and I have a lot of fun together. We go shopping, to the movies, baseball games, and do what ever else I want to do. People tell me that it takes a special person to be friends with someone like Matt. Well I'll tell you something, I don't think I'm a special person. I think Matt is one of the easiest people to be friends with. His fun, outgoing personality makes me want to reach over and hug him.

I just wanted you to know I think you're a great man. You give a lot of encouragement to all people. Thanks for sharing your story with 20/20 so that many people can be educated. Thanks again.

Your New Friend,
Pam Noblet
Bozrah, Connecticut

Dear Mr. Bill,

I just saw your story on 20/20. 1 must tell you that you have given me an inspiration like I have never experienced before. I am 34 years old, and I have been putting myself through college in hopes to get into medical school. I work full time and find it very hard sometimes to complete the complex course work needed to enter medical school. For the past few weeks, I have been thinking about giving up on my dream. Although I have gotten my degree, I still needed to complete a few extra, very difficult classes to prepare myself. With work and lack of money to pay for such classes, I began to get discouraged. But when I saw your story, I realized my problems are minor and my heart was filled with a joy I have never encountered before. I had tears in my eyes when I heard you were struck by a car. I thought I was about to hear you were killed. The world would be a much better place with a lot more Bill Porters. You have given me the inspiration needed to carry on. I feel as though I. have been touched by an Angel and my heart has been lifted. I hope you are doing well this Christmas. I truly thank you from the bottom of my heart for what you have given me.

Merry Christmas

Michael
Baton Rouge, Louisiana

Dear Bill,

I saw you in Winston at the Amway seminar and you were the singular best speaker I have ever heard. You will always remain with me. My grandchild will know you and admire you. You are a blessing from God. All men I have ever known pale in your light. I have always said that your actions are so loud I can't hear what you are saying. You need no microphone, I can hear you every day of my life. As a salesperson, I have been able to overcome a grossly overblown ego with just a glance at your picture. I have been permanently cured of excusitis. How can I best serve you now?

Brian Ethridge
Denver, North Carolina

Dear Mr. Porter,

My name is Milton. I am a petty officer in the U.S. Navy. I am currently stationed at naval station Roosevelt Roads, Puerto Rico.

I am writing you in order to express my admiration for you. I have been asked my whole life who my hero was; who I looked up to. I could never give an answer. I never had anyone that lived up to my expectations of a hero. Now, if anyone asks me who my hero is, I can tell them with pride and certainty, "Mr. Bill Porter of Oregon is my hero."

Thank you, Mr. Porter, for giving me a hero.

Sincerely,
Milton
Ceiba, Puerto Rico

Bill and Shelly,

I heard Bill speak at the Home Base conference in Colorado Springs. My name is Frank Toms, and I am the Marketing Director for Aqua Mix Inc., one of the Home Base's suppliers. I am 32 years old, and I guess you can say I am part of the "me" generation.

It is not often that an individual has changed my attitude/outlook about my life. Bill has shown me the true meaning of spirit, determination, and pride.

Bill, I understand you don't want anyone to feel sorry for you. Based on the accomplishments you have made in your life, I do not pity you. However, please understand that you make perfectly healthy people like myself feel truly blessed for the gifts we were given. I no longer take a lot of things for granted, which in turn has made me a wiser better person. I cannot thank you enough for that wonderful gift.

So, to both of you and your families, I wish you a Merry Christmas.

Frank Toms
Huntington Beach, California

Dear Bill:

I saw you last night for the first time on 20/20. It was a rerun of their original segment on "The Oregonian" story.

It was truly inspirational, Bill. I too am in sales, and know full well how depressing and discouraging this field can be. You however seem to have transcended everything that can discourage a sales representative.

In the first few minutes of the airing, I thought to myself "how much of a disadvantage you must be operating." You see I was thinking of the computer age, the Internet, facsimile technology, etc., not your "so-called" disability.

But as your story continued to unfold, I soon realized that I was missing the point. So often we forget that we are human, we need human touch, feeling, conversation, companionship, to help one another. Whether it be to ask for assistance or — harder yet — allowing ourselves to be helped by others that observe our need and show a willingness to help us.

I guess if there is one thing I appreciate the most about your story it's your total humility. I was touched by you and your life story.

Best wishes to you Bill.

Sincerely,
Barry

P.S. Shelly Brady, you are a very special person, may God continue to bless you.

Dear Bill Porter,

It's Christmas day. Last night I saw your story on 20/20. I was very touched by the kind of person you are, Bill Porter.

In my life I strive every day to think about what I can do to become more influential and have a greater impact on those around me. I think on grand scales — world famous, etc. I think to myself "What can I do in life to become more recognizable and be able to reach more people?" Last night your story gave me the answer. Although not the answer I was necessarily searching for — but an answer nonetheless.

The answer was nothing. I should do nothing but that which I am supposed to do on a daily basis. He who would be King must be servant of all. In my haste to reach some sort of throne in the world, I have forgotten what it is to be lost among the masses doing what I need to do and not worry about who sees me or what consequences may or may not arise because of it.

You are an inspiration — you are a godly man — and you are a King among men.

Then again, you've earned it. God will crown you for the life you have led — your mother, I know, is VERY proud of you.

I hope one day I might meet the man they call Bill Porter.

Aaron Hutchins
Patchogue, New York

Hi!

I saw your story on 20/20 and was moved to loving tears. For me, your story increased my faith in people, especially now when there are so many bad things occurring daily. It must have been meant for me to watch your story because I was just channel flipping. I caught the beginning of the story which I thought was simply about a door-to-door salesman, which just wasn't interesting. But something (that little voice that we should listen to more often) told me to watch it.

Your story also increased my faith, because my life has been horrible because of the sickening wrong doings of others, including parents, family, and people I thought were friends. Daily, I wished I wasn't here, but to see you, Bill, go through every day without complaining taught me a lesson and reminded me of the never ending faith and determination my grandparents had — something I could never understand until now. Thanks for being human — something that the majority of us forget that we are!

Take care and God bless!

Tamra Marie Burgess
Edgewater, New Jersey

And God bless Shelly Brady and her family.

13 Jan, 00

Dear Bill,

Just a note to say hello. Got a nice update from Mrs. Brady. Sorry you haven't been up to par and hope things have improved.

I'm a 63-year-old navy retiree. I've been around a lot of guys in the submarine service and in Vietnam. I've got to say that of all the great veterans and servicemen I've known, that you are on the top of my list for guts and peserverence. I truly admire you and the way you have conducted your life.

I'm certain that some day, far in the future I hope, you will stand before your God, and he will tell you that you are one of his proudest creations. When that time comes, I'm sure your reward will be great.

I wish you the very best, now, and in the days to come. I think you should lighten up some and take it easy. Enjoy the fruits of your excellent labor.

Best wishes.

Lloyd Alfred, USN(SS), Retired
McDonald, Pennsylvania

Mr. Porter,

I first saw your story on 20/20 last year and recorded it based on the promo that they did prior to the show. It brought tears to my eyes. Rarely have I seen that type of media do such a touching and inspiring piece. I suffer from cluster migraine headaches that have ruined my life for 18 years. I no longer feel sorry for myself. Instead, I am ashamed at how much I have blamed my headaches for limiting my options in life. You are a true inspiration, Bill, and I hope someday to shake your hand. I wish you all the best, and a very Merry Christmas (tomorrow). Please take care of yourself, and if you are ever in the area, please let me know via e-mail so I can get that chance to shake your hand and perhaps give you a hug.

If Watkin's could bottle the determination and huge heart you have, I would like very much to purchase some! God bless you, and God bless Shelly for being there for you.

All the best to you.

Max Kane
Gladwin, Michigan

Dear Shelly,

I realize that you are being bombarded with mail. However, I just had to write. I was not there the weekend you and Mr. Porter spoke, but I did see the segment on the news program and heard about you the following weekend at the Convention in Richmond, Virginia.

Mr. Porter is amazing. There have been a couple of people throughout my life with speech impediments. My grandmother was deaf, but still talked in a slurred pattern. God works in amazing ways. Growing up with this helped me understand two different people in college. One was an African from Kenya and had a thick accent. I was able to understand him the first time, so we traded. I helped him with studies and he taught me his language. There was also another person who had CP or MS, and he was easy for me to understand. Also, in my workplace there are people with speech difficulties and it is wonderful to be able to help them when others don't or won't take the time to help.

You are also amazing. With raising a family and still taking time to help this gentleman makes you an Angel in my eyes. When I saw the story a poem that I keep at my desk to remind me daily about a smile and kindness came to mind. I thought I would share it with you.

> My life shall touch a dozen lives before this day is done,
> Leave countless marks for good or ill ere sets the evening sun,
> This is the wish I always wish, the prayer I always pray;

Lord, may my life help others lives it touches by the way.

You and Bill have certainly touched a lot of lives through the Britt Spring Leaderships.

Thank you for letting me share with you and may God be with you and your family.
With Love, Debbie

It is Christmas Eve, and I just finished watching the segment that 20/20 did on your story. I must say that I feel blessed to have turned on the television at the exact time that I did. I am 27, and recently relocated to Ohio from Missouri for my husband's job. My husband is scheduled to go out on the road tomorrow morning at 6:30. He was also working at Thanksgiving, so this will be the second holiday I have spent alone. I must admit that I was feeling very sorry for myself until now. I was both inspired and motivated by your story. I once read that the quality of one's life is not measured by the things one acquires, but by the lives one touches. If this is true (and I am sure it is), then the quality of your life must be immeasurable. I would be willing to bet that your story alone has shaped more lives than you could ever imagine. I am so thankful that you shared your life with others. I will be sure to "count my blessings" more often. Thank you, and have a wonderful Christmas and a SAFE New Year!

Dawn LaRocco
Westerville, Ohio

January 3, 2000

Dear Mr. Porter,

My name is Troy Nelson. I am originally from South Dakota where I was adopted as a baby and raised. I am now 23 years old and have been spending half of my life trying to make a living writing songs. The past few years I have suffered from depression and anxiety which has greatly affected my career choice as a musician. I have been down on myself about my songs and my ability to write them. I always think that I have only a certain time limit before I am too old to be accepted or taken seriously.

After learning about your story of persistence and determination, it has taught me to do what I do and to do it the best that I can do, no matter what people say and that there is no time limit on life when you have a drive that will last forever. After hearing your story, I prayed to God that there is someone like you, an example for all humans. Even though you hear it everyday, and will continue to hear it in the future, THANK YOU.

Sincerely,

Troy M. Nelson
Seattle, Washington

P.S. I am writing a song about your journey and how it's helped me. I would love for you to hear it, and if you do, let me know how I can get it to you. I would be deeply honored.

Wednesday December, 1999

Dear Shelly,

I can't begin to tell you how thankful I am that Bill Porter has an assistant like you. I talked to you on the telephone yesterday for the first time. You are obviously a caring, warm-hearted individual. You have sacrificed in order to help a man who, because of limitations beyond his control, has not had an easy time providing for himself. I can't tell you how much I appreciate that.

I remember Bill Porter. I grew up on Hewett Boulevard in the southwest hills of Portland. Often times, I saw Bill Porter walking from one home to another, not fully aware of his purpose. I certainly was not aware of his history or the daily struggles and challenges he was facing. I have many regrets about not being more perceptive of this man, who is now a daily inspiration both personally and professionally.

I am now 34 years old, married to a wonderful woman, and father of three boys (most recently twin boys who arrived four weeks ago). Like Bill, I am also in sales and have been for the past nine years. Bill Porter has inspired me to be a more thoughtful, self-motivated, and caring individual. My wife, Ingrid, has read the articles about Bill. Together we have watched the program on 20/20. We even ordered a copy of the tape to share with family and friends who missed the program. I can assure you that when my boys are older, they too will know of Bill Porter.

I have saved copies of all the articles I could

find regarding Bill. I have shared his story with all the salespeople that now report to me, as well as our customer service group and management. I took a Dale Carnegie sales course two years ago and shared his story with everyone in the class. His story is a humbling one, and, as you can imagine, put most of the class into tears, which is often times the case when his story is told.

I apologize for the length of the message, but I just wanted you to know how much both of you are appreciated and that you have touched the lives of many. Please take this check and buy something that can be donated to a local charity (i.e., Morrison Center, homeless shelter, women's shelter, etc.). I trust your judgment.

I hope some day to meet Mr. Porter and thank him personally for the positive impact he has had on my life. Until then, please pass along my thanks and best wishes.

Happy Holidays!

Rob Williams
Kent, Washington

Dear Mr. Porter,

I truly enjoyed your recent interview on 20/20. Your story left me so inspired to work hard and NOT complain so much! The next day I told my ten-year-old son about you and he, too, was moved by your story.

Needless to say, my son has been more cooperative with his chores, less procrastinating, and much more attentive. I attribute his new-found maturity much in part to your story and the fine example you are.

Today, my son announced that you were his hero. I wanted you to know.

Most Sincerely,

Hillary Roberts
Keyport, New Jersey

(To learn more about Hillary's nonprofit organization inspired by Bill's story go to www.blankiedepo.org.)

Just wanted to drop by and congratulate you on persevering in a world that is difficult enough for us who's greatest disability is our own attitudes. Saw the segment on 20/20 tonight (Dec. 24) and can only hope to achieve some minute measure of success that you have been able to. You are truly an inspiration to those of us that feel like there is no tomorrow for us in the "selling game." I will face a new year with a different attitude because of you.

Thanks Bill,
John K. Wadsworth
Stockton, California

Dear Bill,

I listened to your story Christmas Eve night on the 20/20 show and had to write you a letter and tell you that your story was an inspiration to me. I work as a police officer in a small town in southern Minnesota, and my wife is a nurse at the state hospital in Fergus Falls, Minnesota. So we both had to go to work Christmas Eve and that's when I had the opportunity to hear about you. I also work at the local high school about two to three days a week and work with kids that are in gangs or come from broken homes or homes without love. I didn't know your mom, Bill, but she was one of those people with an unconditional love. I learned that from hearing your story. I don't think I would have heard about you turning out to be a good person if your mom hadn't been a good person also. I wish these kids I work with had a Mrs. Porter or a Bill Porter in their lives and the world would be a better place.

Bill, if you ever get to Minnesota I am inviting you to the school where I work to share you with the students. I learned once that the meaning of success is getting up one more time after you fall down — BUT now I have a new definition!!!! BILL PORTER!

Well maybe some day I can meet you and sit down and visit with you if you have time. I wish we were closer. Oh by the way, my family also used and sold, for goodness sakes, Watkins Products, and I even think they're from Winona, Minnesota.

Friends Officer,
Jimmy Hansen

Stewart Police Department
Stewart, Minnesota

Dear Bill,

I'm 17 years old and before I went to bed the other night I saw your story on TV. It made me cry very hard. I really admire you for what you have done throughout your life and that you have stuck to it without giving up. I one day hope to have as much determination as you do. It just made me think of what I am going to do with my life and if I'll ever be as determined and happy about what I'm doing as you are. Your story just really made me think a lot. Thank you for sharing it with us!

Missy
Youngsville, North Carolina

12/31/99
Shelly and Bill,

We hope that the New Year brings you health and happiness! I can't help but to say that when I think of you or tell someone your story, Bill, I always seem to say that "I love you" because of who you are! If only I could be half of the person you are! You have touched so many. And Shelly I am very grateful to you that Bill and your lives crossed paths. To know that you have been a longtime friend to him is comforting! He has brought a universal message that the heart is the power of all and that what we "see" is only part of what we get!

Thanks for keeping us posted!
Rhonda & Steve Stenersen
Post Falls, Idaho

Dear Mr. Porter,

Our class viewed your story on 20/20, and was very inspired by your sense of dedication and willingness to press on in life despite the difficulty of the circumstances. Your humble and gentle spirit especially influenced the children, as their letters clearly indicate. You are a person greatly to be admired, and have made a positive and lasting impact on all of the students who have learned of you. I have no doubt that God Himself is greatly appreciative of the many things you have done to make the world a better place. We hope the best of everything for you, as you continue on in your work. You are a blessing to everyone who has come into contact with you.

With great respect and admiration,

Keith
Green Elementary, fifth grade teacher

December 20, 1997

Dear Mr. Bill Porter,

I was watching the ABC News Program 20/20. I was
touched very much by the story about you. You see my
wife and I are mentally handicapped. Both myself,
Greg, and my wife, Val, can walk and talk, but we
don't drive due to our motor coordination, etc. You,
Mr. Porter, have more of a disability than me or my
wife. I am not mad at you. What I am just trying to
say, both my wife and I are adults with learning
disabilities. You have had a hard time in your life,
and the story about you brought tears to our eyes.
You gave us hope and courage that the world of the
disabled can live a normal life, not locked away in
an institution, but in the community of the non-
disabled.

I have a neck-shoulder injury, the story about
you gives me hope to cope with it.

You take care of yourself, I can't think of anything else to say.

Happy Holidays and Thank you,
Greg and Valerie A. Gibson
Somerville, New Jersey

P.S. from my wife, Val: Thank you for making us
realize what we have and how grateful we should be.

December 24, 1997
20/20 News Show
New York, New York

Dear Sir or Madam,

I am compelled to write to you after seeing your story on Bill Porter. He has changed my life. I no longer accept excuses for myself or for others at what they or I can't do, only what I and others can do. I am awe-inspired at what he does on a daily basis without a whine or a complaint. I don't think most people could do this in a lifetime.

His perseverance, determination, and true grit are something to be admired and if more people followed that the world would be a better place. When people talk about hero's, great athletes, movie stars, and politicians come to mind. They don't hold a candle to Bill Porter. For me there is no greater hero than Bill Porter. He is head and shoulders above the rest.

I salute Bill Porter for all that he stands for and I hope that America will take him into their arms and hearts and embrace him too.

I thank you for doing a story on a true hero. I hope you do a follow-up on him so we can all know how he is doing.

Sincerely,

Michelle Solon Rhome
Bardonia, New York

January 2, 1998

Dear Mr. Porter:

We are the family that called you last Sunday. We have two sons, Erik, who is almost 5, and a newborn, Mikal. We showed your story to Erik and he has asked us numerous times since if he could see "that nice man" again. He has asked how you are, and we, as a family, have been praying for you. Every one of us, of whom has been given this gift of life, has been given their own package. Each has special treasures that only that one person can give, and each has their limitations. As a mother, I realize what a gift your mother gave you. She believed in you.

Thank you for allowing 20/20 to share with us your life. It meant a lot to us. Your life is an encouragement to us, and your mothers' life encourages us to instill in our boys that whatever their gifts or talents may be, to put forth their best efforts, and do it with integrity, and to walk humbly before the Lord. In short, we hope to impart in our boys the same sense of determination, perseverance and self-worth that your mother imparted in you.

We pray for your speedy recovery and God's richest blessing on your life.

Sincerely yours, Greg and Angela Winters
Ridgecrest, California

Bill Porter,

I love you! You are my best friend. Thank you for letting us watch your story on T.V. I hope you feel well soon. I love you. God loves you Mr. Bill. I like very much how nice you are to everybody and I like your smile.

Love, Erik

Dear Bill Porter,

I watched the 20/20 that you were on, and I thought it was the best thing that I have ever seen before in my life. I think that you are so courageous. You have a lot of courage to ignore all of the other people and just go on with your dream. That is what I am going to do. I am not going to let anybody tell me that I can't do what my dream may be. I am so happy for you and the way that you are so nice to everybody. I think that whatever you want to do you may do it because you have the courage to do it. I think that that is so cool that you do what you do, I don't think that I could do what you do. All of the other companies that have not let you work for them, I think that they are just plain dumb. I bet that you would and could do much better than the other people selling stuff, way better. You are doing the best job that anybody could ever do. I think that you are doing a good job since you broke your hip. I hope you get better and I think that you should keep up the good work. You should be the leader in everybody's life. You are a great and fantastic role model. Keep up the good work.

From,

Lauren

Dear Bill Porter,

I watched 20/20 in reading class. My name is Erika, and I think you are the greatest nicest person I have ever seen before because you go around the whole town and go to door to door selling things and you are helping people out. I can't believe you can stand being called names or not being excepted at any business place. Even though people say things about you don't care you just keep going on and never stop. You taught kids a lesson and that is to never give up or stop thinking about your dream! And you have inspired me to go for my lifelong dream. You are my guide forever! You have done a good deed for everyone!!!

Sincerely,
Erika

Dear Mr. Porter,

Hello my name is Rachel. You probably don't
know me. The only reason I know you is because I
just saw your story on 20/20. It made me cry. I am
10 years old. I can't believe you never give up. You
should be happy for that. Because if I were you I'd
give up. Also you don't take no for an answer. Now
that is amazing. You know what if you still have
trouble hearing you can buy hearing aids.

Yours truly,
Rachel
P.S. Call me

December 24, 1997

ABC-TV - 20/20
New York, New York

To Whom It May Concern:

Rarely does a television program move me emotionally as much as the "Bill Porter" segment of the 20/20 program did almost two weeks ago. Before the show was over, I knew I had to do something to create positive reinforcement of desired behavior. I wrote down the name of the segment and the employer of Mr. Porter as well as his hometown. With the Christmas season in full swing, I did not have the time to begin this letter and the others I will write until today.

I don't believe I have ever written to a television station to compliment them on their programming. This is primarily because I do not believe the majority of programming on any of the major networks is worthy of compliments. However, with the broadcast of the "Bill Porter" segment, it is apparent that there is still hope.

Bill Porter embodies all of the good qualities of human nature we all should strive to possess. He is an excellent example for anyone to follow. From an employers perspective, he is dependable, loyal, driven, motivated, confident, selfless, conscientious, talented, dedicated, and the list goes on and on. From a human perspective he embodies all of these same traits and is caring, concerned, loving, a friend to all, and a good citizen and neighbor. He is the man I hope to be and want my kids to grow up to be like. He is Bill Porter in spite all of his physical deviations from the norm. His heart is clearly visible through the way he lives his life.

Bill Porter reminds me of my dad with his work ethic. He doesn't feel society owes him anything and he works hard for what he has.

While I watched this segment, my emotions welled up inside of me and escaped as tears of joy. I was so overwhelmed with how truly exceptional this man is without even considering his physical differences. We need for all stations to find the Bill Porter's of the world and feature their lives in segments or documentaries like yours. This is the programming we need for our fathers, mothers, and children to see and having seen, hopefully strive to develop the qualities Bill Porter has. Your station is to be commended on this quality piece of work and encouraged to replace the garbage that permeates all daily programming with human-interest stories like this. I cannot remember a program that has so stirred my inner being as much as this one. It motivated me to get off the couch and do something. I'm sure I am not alone in that regard.

I cannot say enough about the quality of this piece. I want to personally thank those responsible for the Bill Porter piece for doing such an excellent job showcasing one of America's truly great resources, Bill Porter.

Thanks again and Happy Holidays!

With best regards, I am Sincerely yours,
William M. Magee
Abita Springs, Louisiana

Cc: NBC-TV; CBS-TV; FOX-TV; The Watkins Company; Bill Porter; The Learning Channel; The Discovery Channel

January 19, 1998
Dear Mr. Porter,

I have been meaning to sit down to write you
this letter since I first heard your story on 20/20
in December. I even looked up the program informa-
tion on the 20/20 website pages and printed it out
(with photos) as a reminder of a remarkably courageous person.

I would simply like to thank you for allowing
your story to be told. I understand from the tele-
cast that you were somewhat reluctant. Let me just
say that your story, Mr. Porter, has changed the way
I look at myself and for this I want to thank you.

I once read that courage is the most important
virtue because without it you can't do anything else
with consistency. You, Mr. Porter, are living proof
and the embodiment of all, that I believe, "courage"
means.

I too have been waging a war against the odds —
for almost twelve years now I have been battling
cancer. A mere drop in the bucket though, when com-
pared to your sixty-five years. I am not, however,
courageous like you. What an incredible gift you
possess to have been such a fighter, such a doer,
such an incredibly strong being, right from the
beginning. I wasn't diagnosed with cancer until I
was 37 years old. Up until that time I never really
understood how precious this life is. Well, I almost
lost sight of that until I was lucky enough to catch
20/20 that Friday night — when I saw you.

Your story has touched me in a way that I find
hard to explain. I think you know what I mean
though, Mr. Porter. Just the mere fact that the segment on you drew the largest response of any story

in 20/20's history is a testament of how many lives you touched.

Again, thank you, Mr. Porter, for taking the time to share your life. You will always be an inspiration to me, especially at those times when I don't feel like fighting cancer anymore. Just thinking about you will set things right.

God's speed, Mr. Porter. Stay well. It's like I keep telling my oncologist — it's so much more than medicine.

With deepest regards,

Maryann Wells
Streetsville, Ontario, Canada

December 14, 1997

Dear Bill,

Enjoyed seeing the piece on you on 20/20. My heart swelled with pride for the accomplishment in your life. The great satisfaction you must take in making your own way in the world.

My oldest brother is now 55 and suffered from an injury at birth. He still lives with our mother in Ohio. Mother is now 78. Sonny never developed the power of speech or fine motor skills, like buttoning buttons or zipping a zipper. He has spent his life in my parents home being loved and well cared for. The past 15 years he has been able to go to a sheltered workshop. The bus picks him up every morning and drops him off late in the afternoon. The thought of being self-sufficient, holding a job would have been but a dream, but he remains sweet and pleasant — just like you. Your goodness and kindness came shining through!!!

Through my brother I have a sincere sense of your accomplishments. How proud your mother would have been. My best wishes and good thoughts go out to you on this Christmas holiday.

I've included a small gift for under your tree.

Steve Graumlich
Savannah, Georgia

Dear Bill,

I was thrilled to see you on 20/20 on TV. It seems like just yesterday when we were going to Grout Center. I am certainly glad you were able to be a salesman as you always wanted to be. I am sorry to hear about your mother. As I remember her, she was a very wonderful lady, as were all our mothers. You remember I lost my mother shortly after I graduated from Grout. Those were hard days. As I remember you went to the Salvation Army Camp right after school was out in 1950. I don't remember if you were there in 1951 or not. That is the last time I had significant contact with any of the students that went to Grout Center. My dad remarried then in September of 1950. After I graduated from Grout, I was able to attend Franklin High School and graduate in 1954. I was able to graduate from Brigham Young University in chemistry and also graduate from the University of Utah Law School. I worked in the United States Patent Office as a Patent Examiner until 1990 when I had to retire on disability because my spinal cord was compromised, parazlying my arms. I have been living in Utah since 1990.

The Lord has blessed me with a family and a career. We are both so fortunate that we were able to accomplish something with our lives and fit into society. It must have been a struggle for you to keep up your sales route. It seems now that handicapped people have the attitude they want to be compensated for their handicap. I think both of us have struggled to give something to society and to do the best we can with our handicap. I have had a

lot of help from people and I imagine you have too.
I have not demanded help and it saddens me that
some of the people in the handicapped movement
demand accommodations that are unreasonable.

Have you kept track of any of the kids we knew?
I have completely lost track of everyone. I have
seen David Ingerson and Neil Firm in Portland
three times in the past thirty years. As I remember
it, they were on the staff of the CP Center in south-
east Portland. I think the last time I had any contact was in 1979 or 1980. I heard Janie Poor and
Morris Foss got married. Do you ever see them? My
wife is typing this letter for me, and if it is too
difficult for you to write to me, don't worry about
it. If you are able to give me a call, we might be
able to understand each other. I am out of practice,
however, and the general public has trouble understanding me at times. My phone number is in the
evening.

Delbert Phillips
Springville, Utah

A
F
T
E
R
W
O
R
D

by **Bill Porter**

To me, the thought that others will find my life worthy of an entire book is unbelievable. Even more unbelievable is this beautiful book that Shelly has written. When she asked me if I had anything to add to the book, my answer was "You bet. I want to thank all the people who have contributed to my life story."

So many people have helped me throughout my life and made my life better. I wish I could thank each and every one of them, but I can't. My gratitude to them is so great that it would take me years and years just to express it, so a simple thank you will have to suffice.

Many people have been generous with gifts, such as Mark and Lizzette Rolls of Primerica Financial Services who gave us a trip to Disneyland. Others have given me the gift of time. Father Arthur Dernbach, the priest at Saint Thomas More Catholic Church in Portland, was always there to talk with me and advise me. The church secretaries and members were always kind and welcoming to me, too. I ate my lunch in the churchyard every day for years, and Father Dernbach would join me and we would sit and chat. Later, when Mother was ill and passed away, Father Dernbach performed the memorial funeral service and everyone in the congregation comforted me through my sorrow and loss.

Shelly deserves my thanks for all the help she has given me over the years, and especially for helping me tell my story. I appreciate the Brady family's generosity in sharing her with me and for being my "family," too. Thanks to all the people who saw my story in the newspaper or on television and sent me letters. My biggest thank you, though, goes to my customers whose orders, small and large, made my life possible.

I never thought my life had meaning, and I didn't live it as though it was important to anyone except those close to me. My message to everyone who reads this book is that your life is important, too. Think about each person you meet each day of your life and what effect you might have upon them, for good or ill. It isn't always the big decisions that make a difference in our lives; more often, it's the little ones. The extra smile or wave; calling a friend who is ill; going out of your way to help someone whether they ask or not. Each of you has the same opportunity to inspire others as I do, simply by living your life as best you can. People tell me that I have touched thousands of lives, but what I think is that hundreds and thousands of people have helped me. Thank you, each of you, and every time you ask yourself if you can make a difference, remember this answer: You bet you can.

LIST OF ILLUSTRATIONS

ACKNOWLEDGMENTS

There are so many people I wish to express my appreciation to, so many who have taught me great lessons in teamwork, friendship, and support. My greatest fear is that I will miss someone. If I do I hope that they will forgive me and know they are in my heart.

My greatest blessing, love, and joy come from my family. I am so thankful for a patient, loving husband. John has supported me all the years as I have delivered Watkins products, shopped, and cleaned for Bill (even when we had no clean clothing or milk in our own fridge). He's lovingly cared for our children while I flew around the country inspiring others with Bill's story. He's kindly picked up countless pizzas on his way home from work when time and again I didn't get around to fixing dinner while working on this book. He's helped me figure out how to balance my role as a homemaker with my speaking career. He's also encouraged and helped me with ideas for this book. He is my best friend.

My children mean the world to me: Michelle, Katrina,

Teressa, Kevin, Erica, and Emily. I appreciate their continuous support and patience with me. (One daughter has informed me that when she grows up, she wants to be a mom, but she won't write a book. She'll just play with her children.) They cooked, cleaned, played with the ones briefly missing mommy, and changed the baby's diapers when I was out of town or locked away in my room writing. They love me unconditionally. For the past several years, they, along with their father, helped deliver Bill's products. They help me clean Bill's house. They bring me great joy. They are my greatest moments!

I love and appreciate my mother, Harriette Hankel, so much. She is the busiest person I know but always takes the time to listen to me. She has spent hours reading every chapter over and over, offering her suggestions.

To all my parents — Gary (Dad), Linda, John, and Harriette (Mom) — thanks for helping me grow up.

To my sisters and brothers — Ann, Shayne, Chris, Che, Israel, Glenn, and Jennifer — thank you for always being there. To Che for making me promise if I ever wrote this book that some of the proceeds should be earmarked to help someone else, resulting in New World Library's contribution to United Cerebral Palsy.

I could not have written this book or traveled with Bill without the help of my "team." To my in-laws, Elwood and Melba Brady, thank you for lovingly tending your grandchildren — my babies — so many times over the past few years. It's comforting to know my children are in the best of hands when I am gone or busy at the computer.

Thanks also to Diane Young and Sheila Painter, friends as close as family, who also spent countless hours tending my little ones so I could travel or work on this book.

I mention with gratitude the many friends who helped me with the book by reading, proofing, and sharing their thoughts and ideas with me: Wendi Stephens, Tesa Stephens, Polly Johnson, Rhonda Carter, and Tricia Craft. Thank you so much for your help and thank you most of all for your friendship.

I would like to thank everyone at Nationwide Speakers Bureau, especially our agent, Dan Savage, for representing Bill and me these past few years and opening doors for us to speak all over this great country to people from all over this great world.

To our good friend Robert J. King, who got the ball rolling for the most amazing movie project ever! To Carey Nelson-Burch who hooked Rob up with Dan Angel, Billy Brown, and Forest Whitaker who helped roll that ball faster and faster. To everyone at TNT, including producers David A. Rosemont and Warren Carr, who made it happen. To Steven Schachter who helped write the screenplay and directed the movie *Door to Door*. To the actors and crew on the set of the movie who poured their hearts into their work. And last but not least, to William H. (Bill) Macy who co-wrote and starred as my friend Bill Porter in the movie. To all of these wonderful people, thanks for seeing Bill's story as the wonderful piece of life that it is and for making a movie that will touch millions. And thanks, Bill Macy, for writing the foreword to this book, for sitting in a make-up chair for hours each day, for capturing the spirit and heart of Bill Porter as you played him, and for being our friend.

I would like to thank Katie Farnam Conolly, Georgia Hughes, Monique Muhlenkamp, Mary Ann Casler, and all the wonderful team of people at New World Library. Thank you for taking me by the hand and leading me through the amazing world of crafting a book. Thanks for your vision. Thanks for the hours of editing, designing, and creative juices poured into this work. Bill and I are forever grateful. And thank you for hooking me up with Eric Bolt.

To Eric Bolt, my developmental editor, thank you for the hours, days, weeks, and months of e-mails and phone calls aiding me along the journey of writing Bill's inspirational story. Thank you for cutting, pasting, dressing up, and trimming down. Thank you for pushing me to pull stories locked inside and helping me express them in the best way possible.

I want to thank God for all of my many blessings including my friends and family mentioned and those not mentioned but in my heart. Most of all, I want to thank God whose hand, I believe, led our various paths to intersect. I am grateful to Him that my path crossed Bill Porter's so long ago. I am thankful that Bill hired me, didn't fire me, and eventually became my friend. Thank you, Bill, for your courageous, inspiring life. Thank you Bill, for being you.